BUILDING ACCORDING TO THE DIVINE PATTERN

Israel Onoriobe

Building According To The Divine Pattern

ISBN: 978-0-620-66691-6

Apostle Israel Onoriobe
World Vision Crusade Outreach Ministries
9 Pegasus Road,
Milnerton, Cape Town - South Africa
Tel: +27 21 828 2345
Mobile: +27 82 228 9180
Email: wvcom2001@yahoo.com

Visit Us Online
@
www.wvcom-international.org

Unless otherwise indicated, all scripture quotations are taken from the King James Version (KJV) of the Holy Bible.
Any emphasis in quoted scripture is mine.

Graphic Design by: Afilok Designers
Tel: +27 78 232 6974 - Email: design@afilok.org
Website: www.afilok.org .

Table Of Content

Acknowledgement

I give thanks to God the Father, to the Lord Jesus Christ, and to the Holy Spirit for the wisdom, revelation and understanding to write this work, for whom and through whom everything exists, to build His Church according to His pattern for His habitation.

A special thanks also to my editor in Australia, Mary Gray, for her good work, and the sacrifice to edit this book at the Nursing Home while caring for her husband, Lew. May the Lord bless and strengthen you.

Dedication

This book is dedicated to leaders globally in the Body of Christ who are in pursuit of God's original purpose - (the kingdom of God), and to those whose heart are earnestly seeking to build all things according to the pattern of God.

Introduction

It was in April 2015 while on a mission trip that I felt the need to write this book. I was ministering at a fellowship in Brisbane, Australia and the theme for that conference was tagged "Building According To Divine Pattern". The Church fellowship was going through a turbulent time as they were rebuilding and restructuring things to establish order.

Out of this experience in helping the Church in Australia, and through further teachings and ministry in several churches and nations, the Lord began to open my understanding to this pattern and process for building His house which I have laid down in this book.

"See to it that you make everything according to the pattern shown you on the mountain" - (Hebrews 8:5b NIV).

It is not building that is important, but building accurately. Heaven must be reflected on earth. The pattern must be a foreshadowing of what has its true existence and reality in the heavenly sanctuary.

The pattern of God must be followed in its completeness and comprehensiveness, with all its particularity of detail in order to be true to what He is building in and through us. To achieve this, there must be a clear understanding of the purposes of God, His pattern and the order He has set.

As we seek to build accurately according to the pattern of God, it is important to know that this cannot be done without the Holy Spirit. He is the only Person that can reveal the Builder (Jesus Christ) and the pattern of God to us. The Holy Spirit is the only One that can enable us to build by this pattern.

Without the Holy Spirit we cannot know Jesus Christ – the Builder (Matthew 16:18), and the Father, because He is the One that can reveal Him to us – John 15:26.

Without the Holy Spirit we cannot understand His Kingdom, because He is the agent of revelation. He is the One who bears witness of Jesus who is the King of the Kingdom - Romans 14:17.

Without the Holy Spirit we cannot receive or understand His pattern. He is the One that reveals the pattern of the heaven to us for the building of the house of God (the Body of Christ) - 1 Chronicles 28:12, 1 Corinthians 2:10-14, Ephesians 2:22.

Without the Holy Spirit we cannot know our primary assignment to influence our spheres and make impact - Romans 15:19.

Without the Holy Spirit we cannot fulfill the will and purposes of God, because He is the One that enables us. He is the grace of God that is at work in us, and through us - Acts 1:8.

The Holy Spirit is the One that guides us into all truth, out from religion, laws and traditions of men - John 16:13, Romans 8:1-11, Galatians 5:18.

Without the Holy Spirit, nothing that we build or do will be pleasing and acceptable to the Father. It becomes dead works.

My goal is to further equip you to:
Know The Lord – Growing In Your Relationship.
Know His Purpose – Be Established In His Will.
Know Your Assignment – Fulfilling Your Calling.

That 'knowing', will enable you to embrace the basics and to position yourself to model the principles and pattern of the kingdom of God.

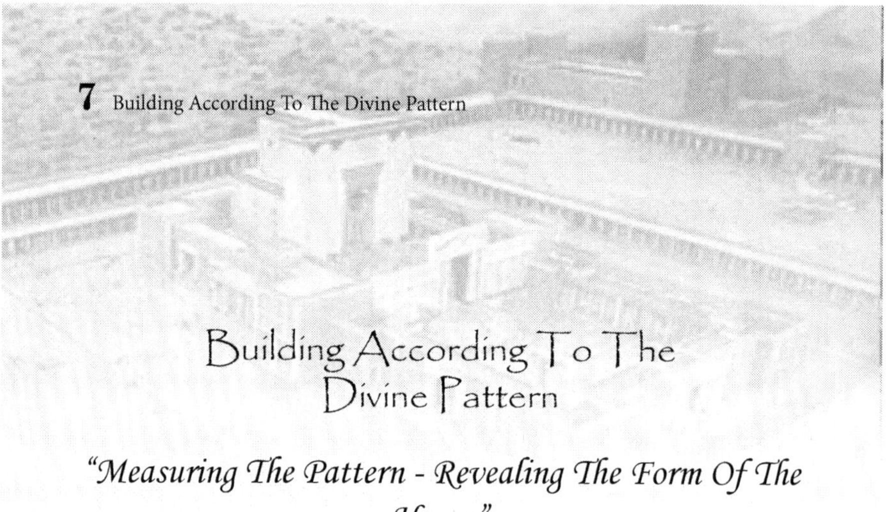

7 Building According To The Divine Pattern

Building According To The Divine Pattern

"Measuring The Pattern - Revealing The Form Of The House"

"Thou son of man, shew the house to the house of Israel, that they may be ashamed of their iniquities: and let them measure the pattern. And if they be ashamed of all that they have done, shew them the form of the house, and the fashion thereof, and the goings out thereof, and the comings in thereof, and all the forms thereof, and all the ordinances thereof... and all the laws thereof: and write it in their sight, that they may keep the whole form thereof, and all the ordinances thereof, and do them." - **(Ezekiel 43:10-11).**

Chapter One

Building According To The Divine Pattern

A new season has dawned upon us and it is imperative that we clearly understand God's purpose and accurately align ourselves to His will. Like the sons of Issachar, we must not only understand the significance of the present time we are living in by keeping up-to-date, we must also know what to do as required of the Lord.

"The tribe of Issachar supplied 200 leaders....They kept up-to-date in their understanding of the times and knew what Israel should do" - (1Chronicles 12:32 ISV).

As we approach the end of the age we must not loose focus on the goal of God and that which He seeks to accomplish. God's purpose is to build Himself a house, a dwelling place among His people. God's ultimate goal from the beginning of the ages is to tabernacle (dwell/live) among His people forever.

God is immutable – He is the same yesterday, today and forever. He is an unchangeable God. His plans and purposes are still the same as they were from the beginning of the age. The seasons of God's visitations are fading away, because God no longer wants to be visiting His people; His desire is to dwell among them. This has been His desire and His purpose from the beginning.

"And let them make me a sanctuary; that I may dwell among them" - (Exodus 25:8).

The prophetic revelatory verdict of His proclamation and intent is, *"the dwelling place of God is among humans, and He will tabernacle with them, and they shall be His people, and God Himself shall be with them, and He will be their God"* - Revelation 21:3.

The sanctuary was the house of God, which was His dwelling place among His people in the Old Testament. The sanctuary in the Old Testament is symbolic, and it is a shadow or a reflection of the house of God in the New Testament. **The house of God in the New Testament is the Church. The Church is *now* the sanctuary of God.**

Paul the apostle of the Lord Jesus in his letter to young Timothy (his son in the faith) wrote, '....the house of God, which is the church of the living God, the pillar and ground of the truth' - 1 Timothy 3:15.

If the Church of the living God is the house of God, then it must be built according to God's divine pattern just as God instructed Moses to see to it that the sanctuary was built according to the pattern He showed him.

"Exactly as I show you concerning the pattern of the tabernacle, and of all its furniture, so you shall make it" - (Exodus 25:9 ESV).

We must faithfully and accurately build according to the pattern - the blue print as it is clearly revealed in the New Testament, if we are to be a true reflection of the New Covenant Church that God desires to establish on earth for His purpose and kingdom. Anything we have built other than that which has been revealed by the Lord to us in the scriptures is not the pattern, and it will not have the blessing and glory of God.

Speaking of the Church, we are not talking about a physical building or an organizational structure that is to be built, but we are talking about an organism of a called-out people who have and are responding to a heavenly call - This is known as the Ecclesia of God.

The Church is not a building. It is not a denomination. It is not a religious organization. The Church is a corporate people known as the Body of Christ. We are the temple of the Lord, and the Spirit of God dwells in us - 1 Corinthians 3:16, 1 Corinthians 6:19, 1 Corinthians 12:27.

The Church (Ecclesia) is not something that is built by a human system. So many man-made systems and structures have invaded the Church. What we have called the Church has been a social gathering with some spiritual proclivity. Some of the visions have been men's ambition. We have bought into a babylonian system and clothed it with a fangled robe and called it the Church.

Babylon is a false religious system of men and of this world; a counterfeit of the spiritual system of the Church and of the divine order of God in heaven. This false religious system of babylon is masterminded by the devil to spiritually hold people captive against the system of heaven. Babylon is a system of the antichrist because it is legalistic, perverse, controlling and manipulating. It depraves the mind of people against God's pattern.

Interestingly our perspective and way is not always a reflection of the divine pattern of God, even though we have good plans and intentions and we are sometimes convinced that it is the Lord, who has led us or given us the vision. Our mind must be aligned to a true kingdom understanding and revelation in order to see things perfectly with the eyes of the Spirit and to walk therein.

"Don't copy the behaviour and customs of this world, but let God transform you into a new person by changing the way you think. Then you will learn to know God's will for you, which is good and pleasing and perfect." - (Romans 12:2 NLT).

The renewal of our mindset will transform us into a new person which will help us to know the will of God and to see things the way the Lord has ordered it, so we can build according to His pattern. We cannot continue to walk with an old mindset and expect to fulfill the purposes of God in this new season. *Walking with an Egypt mentality will never produce an inheritor of a Promised Land people.* The mind of the builders must be transformed in order to percieve accurateky and to build according to the divine pattern of God.

Until all things are done according to God's pattern as He has revealed, His presence and His glory will be absent. The whole purpose for building according to the divine pattern of God is to make a place for God to dwell. Except this is done accurately His presence and His glory will not abide. <u>If we want to see the fullness of God's glory and power at work in the Church and in the nations, then the Divine Order of God must be set in place</u>.

One of the ways God builds according to His pattern is to shake things around us; the things that remain cannot be removed and the things that cannot be removed are eternal. The shaking of God is part of God's pattern to develop us to become a people and the Church that He intends for us to be.

"See that ye refuse not Him that speaketh. For if they escaped not who refused him that spake on earth, much more shall not we escape, if we turn away from Him that speaketh from heaven: Whose voice then shook the earth: but now He hath promised, saying, Yet once more I shake not the earth only, but also heaven. And this word, Yet once more, signifieth the removing of those things that are shaken, as of things that are made, that those things which cannot be shaken may remain. Wherefore we receiving a kingdom which cannot be moved, let us have grace, whereby we may serve God acceptably with reverence and godly fear" - (Hebrews 12:25-28).

God is shaking the earth and the heaven in order for the things that are not eternal, which are not built according to His pattern, to be removed. The temporal things are permissive, but they are not part of the eternal purposes of God. The Father in this season is shaking and removing them so there can be a true reflection of the heavenly things on earth.

God is shaking the nations. God is shaking the Church. God is shaking doctrines. Systems are being shaken to produce an unshakable people. This shaking is a divine process to produce an unshakable people who are established in His kingdom that cannot be removed. The unshakable things are the eternal things that are built according to His pattern. These are the holy things.

We must note the emphasis of the writer of the book of Hebrews saying, '....*Yet once more, signifieth the removing of those things that are shaken, as of things that are made*'.

The myopic character and mindset of the 'until death commitment' we hold in regard to our man-made traditions will be radically shaken by God. Man-made systems and elements; the doctrines and traditions of men which do not reflect the eternal purposes of God that have been made and established within the Church, will be removed because they have held the people of God under bondage.

God is a God of Order. God is a God of Process. God is a God of Pattern. The establishment of God's order, process and pattern in us will produce an unshakable people. The more we associate ourselves with God's way and pattern it will produce an unshakable kingdom within us, and the Church. This calls for a whole new walk with the Lord that requires us to know Him. The more we know Him, the more we will want to know Him, and the more we want to know Him, He will reveal His pattern and His ways to us.

The focal point of the New Covenant is that God seeks for a people that will know Him. To achieve this, He renders the old pattern and the old way (Old Covenant) obsolete, and imparts a new mindset and pattern that will revolutionize the heart of a people to seek Him, and to continue in a new and better way.

"For this is the covenant that I will make with the house of Israel after those days, saith the Lord; I will put my laws into their mind, and write them in their hearts: and I will be to them a God, and they shall be to me a people: And they shall not teach every man his neighbour, and every man his brother, saying, Know the Lord: for all shall know me, from the least to the greatest.....In that He saith, A new covenant, He hath made the first old. Now that which decayeth and waxeth old is ready to vanish away" - (Hebrews 8:10-11, 13).

To build according to pattern is to operate in Due Order, to do things according to the rule of God; the way He designated it to be from the foundation.

We need to understand that in the midst of all that God is doing there is a "Due Order" for things to be done. David's transportation of the Ark is one such example. ***David was hearing accurately - but his approach with the people was inaccurate.*** They were responding to the sound of a new voice, and a divine direction from God, but with their own way of doing things, which was clearly a violation of God's pattern.

The Ark of the Covenant is symbolic of God's throne established upon the earth. It represented the dwelling of God and His presence among His people. When the Ark was set in its place and its pattern fully observed, it brought blessings, protection, happiness and peace to the people of God.

King David knew the importance of the Ark of the Covenant in its rightful place in the kingdom. Although he was a strong prophetic king that understood the heart desire of God - a man whose heart was after the Lord, and the need to bring the ark to Zion, but he missed the divine pattern of God as he journeyed to transport the ark to Zion.

The Due Order the Lord had set for the Ark of the Covenant was given to Moses on the Mount. It was the order of the tabernacle and of the Levitical priesthood, which Aaron was set in place and commissioned as the first High Priest in Israel, with his four sons to take responsibility over the ark. The bearing of the Ark had to be on the shoulders, and it is only the Levitical priests that had this responsibility. This was the pattern the Lord had ordered.

"But unto the sons of Kohath he gave none: because the service of the sanctuary belonging unto them was that **they should bear upon their shoulders**" - (Numbers 7:9).

But David and his men went and carried the Ark of the Covenant on a ***new cart*** which was a violation of the way and pattern the Lord had designated from the beginning. As a result of this, the Lord made a breach upon them on their way at the threshingfloor of Chidon because the oxen was released and stumbled. Uzza was killed as the anger of the Lord was kindled against him, because he put his hand on the Ark to hold it from falling.

"And David went up, and all Israel, to Baalah, that is, to Kirjathjearim, which belonged to Judah, to bring up thence the ark of God the LORD, that dwelleth between the cherubims, whose name is called on it. And they carried the ark of God in a new cart out of the house of Abinadab: and Uzza and Ahio drave the cart. And David and all Israel played before God with all their might, and with singing, and with harps, and with psalteries, and with timbrels, and with cymbals, and with trumpets. And when they came unto the threshingfloor of Chidon, Uzza put forth his hand to hold the ark; for the oxen stumbled. And the anger of the LORD was kindled against Uzza, and He smote him, because he put his hand to the ark: and there he died before God. And David was displeased, because the LORD had made a breach upon Uzza: wherefore that place is called Perezuzza to this day" - (1 Chronicles 13:6-11).

As a result of the breach the Lord made upon Uzza, king David had to abort that mission for non compliance to the pattern for the next three months. He had to observe the pattern of God in order to bring the Ark of the Covenant into its rightful place at Zion, and there was great joy and peace afterward.

"Then David said, None ought to carry the ark of God but the Levites: for them hath the LORD chosen to carry the ark of God, and to minister unto Him for ever. And David gathered all Israel together to Jerusalem, to bring up the ark of the LORD unto his place, which he had prepared for it. And David assembled the children of Aaron, and the Levites:" - (1 Chronicles 15:2-4).

I recommend that a full study be made on the following chapters of 1 Chronicles chapters 12, 13 and 15, to fully understand the process of transition that was taking place from the old order of things under the administration of king Saul, who is a type of the church operating under an inaccurate pattern; to a new order of things under the leadership of king David, who is a type of a true kingdom Church being established in divine pattern.

It is important to note that David's good intention was for the ark to be brought back into the kingdom so that they might seek the Lord at it, but his method was wrong. Good intention does not necessarily produce God intention. A wrong method cannot produce a right result. When things are out of order, it always hits a bump on the road.

When things are done according to the way and the rule God has originally designed them to be, then His presence and His blessings will begin to manifest and be established. This will always bring great joy and gladness of heart. This is when our true purpose in Him is accomplished.

Anything that is done without the Due Order and pattern of God's way, and His rule will always require the strength of a man (Uzza) to hold and sustain it, but the ultimate reality is that it will eventually stumble like the Ark and bring death. Uzza put forth his hand to hold the Ark to help sustain and keep it as the oxen stumbled, because the pattern of God was not followed. The Greek word for "Uzza" means 'the strength of a man'.

They built a new cart, hitched it up to some oxen (a type of the flesh or beast nature) and Uzza (strength) and Ahio (his brother) were elected to drive the cart. That was a representation of Man's Best Effort with the Flesh Nature – Beast! So the Lord intervenes and kills Uzza (Strength) as he tries to save the Ark of God in his own strength.

The fascinating part is that Uzza and Ahio were Levites and sons of Abinadab who was the priest. The Ark has been in their home for years (2 Samuel 6:3-4). Without doubt they have been accustomed to the precise instructions regarding the Ark. You would expect Uzza to have known the pattern for the house and for the Ark, but unfortunately he was carried away by the busyness of the program and the noise of the day, and he walked in an inaccurate manner that resulted to his death as God made a breach on the program.

We should not become so familiar with the eternal things of God that we now have an irreverent attitude towards the way of God, because this will place our lives at risk. Our heart must always be humble to seek for God's pattern and to do according to His will. All that is needed is obedience. We cannot replace obedience with ministry. We must have an accurate understanding of what God has said, so we know what He is saying now in order to fulfill it. It is absolute disobedient to the order of God to operate things in our own way. Obedience is to seek the truth of God and His kingdom, and walk in them without compromise.

So many church leaders are trying to sustain their church ministry and denominational organization through their in-built programs and church growth system, which is a borrowed Babylonian system of man's way of doing things to reach God. This is the implementation of the human strength to help sustain our stumbling work which is inaccurate in this present season. Most of these ministries are dead churches and organizations, and all they do is to try to revive it by wasting resources to bring well known preachers with some kind of influence to speak, or with some fancy business strategies they promote through the media. This is because they have failed to realize that they have missed God's pattern, and He has made a breach upon them and their self kingdoms which they have built.

God will build His Church that will operate with the keys of the kingdom of heaven; He will not build ***your*** church (Matthew 16:18-19).

We must stop working things out in our own way and in our human strength. It is imperative that we seek to do things by divine pattern. The failure to do so is one of the primary causes of the delay of God's purpose among us in every aspect of the Church and our lives, and its fruit is a circumvented mandate and destiny which is hijacked by carnal men and demonic forces prevailing against us.

David inquired of the Lord and received the "Due Order" for transporting the Ark, which was on the shoulders of the priests, and he walked in that pattern and there was a restoration of God's righteousness and order in his kingdom.

Another important aspect in the establishment of God's pattern which was seen with king David and the Ark of the Covenant as things were being done according to Due Order; is the call for sanctification.

"And (David) said unto them, Ye are the chief of the fathers of the Levites: **sanctify yourselves,** both ye and your brethren, that ye may bring up the ark of the LORD God of Israel unto the place that I have prepared for it" - (1 Chronicles 15:12).

God's divine order and pattern cannot be fully established in a church or in any aspect of our lives and societal spheres until we are sanctified.

To be sanctified is to be cleansed (to make holy), and to be set apart from the old ways and inaccurate patterns.

(A) Be Cleansed - The things of the past that are not of the eternal purposes of God must be cleansed from us. They must go away forever. This is the preserving of the sense of God's holiness and fear as we are being prepared for Him.

(B) Be Set Apart - We must be separated from the former things, and be set apart as a holy people dedicated to God.

To be sanctified is "two ways". Firstly, we are cleansed (*something is removed from us*), and secondly we are set apart (*we are removed from something*). All things must be ratified in God's pattern.

"Depart! Depart! Go out from there; touch no unclean thing; go out from the midst of her; purify yourselves, you who carry the vessels of the LORD" - (Isaiah 52:11).

God's glory cannot be embodied in an unclean vessel. The Holy Spirit or the anointing will not flow through an unclean ministry because it will corrupt the purity of the anointing. There is a special Holy anointing that God has reserved only for those He has called for His Holy service. God will not pour this Holy anointing upon any strange ministry, and those that tries to copy and compound the anointing, the judgement of God will rest upon them. The anointing is not poured upon ALL flesh (unclean human nature or carnality) - Exodus 30:22-33.

We must be clean (holy) in order to carry the Lord's holy items. <u>Holiness is a requirement for God's house</u>.

"Wherefore gird up the loins of your mind, be sober, and hope to the end for the grace that is to be brought unto you at the revelation of Jesus Christ; As obedient children, not fashioning yourselves according to the former lusts in your ignorance: But as He which hath called you is holy, so be ye holy in all manner of conversation; Because it is written, Be ye holy; for I am holy" - (1 Peter 1:13-16).

There is a song lyrics that says:

Lord, prepare me to be a sanctuary
Pure and holy, tried and true
With thanksgiving, I'll be a living
Sanctuary for You

There is a need for us to prepare our bodies and minds as a living sacrifice for the Lord. To build according to God's pattern, we must not only have a clear vision and revelation of the blue print (pattern), but we must also have the right attitude of heart. The motive of our heart must be pure and set in order with God's will for us to be able to build as a wise master-builder.

I have been blessed with the privilege of travelling to over 44 nations in all the continents of the earth for the fulfillment of God's purpose. This has allowed me the opportunity to experience different cultures and lifestyles among the people and Church fellowship. The interesting part as it relates to this subject, is that I have always seen some of these dear brethren doing things to honor the grace of God upon me during my visit as they go out of their way to prepare a place for me to dwell. They always clean the room, and on several occasions I have even seen them replaced their bedding and furniture with new ones because of my stay in their home. To them it is considered a privilege of being honored for a messenger of God to come from a far country to live with them. If they could think to prepare in this manner and do this for me, how much more are we as a Church to prepare our bodies and minds as a living sacrifice for the Lord to make Him a suitable habitation in us. What a royal privilege to have God coming to live in and among us. I will not trade this for anything!

As a new season of reformation has dawned upon us, let us align ourselves to the way of God and build according to His pattern. God is building His house - the Church, and it must be done according to His pattern. Anything done less than His pattern will never produce His purpose or bring His glory.

The scenario with king David and the ark is a reminder to today's emerging Church and leaders that one can have a strong emphasis on the prophetic ministry gift and the message of the kingdom, but still fall short in building an apostolic foundation and pattern.

God's due order was that the *only* people permitted to carry the Ark of the Covenant were those connected in a Levitical family way and a sonship way to their priestly father. The pattern was Aaron and his four sons with him, who were permitted to carry the Ark.

King David realized that he had not done things after the Due Order. He had to return back to the pattern the Lord established in the Levitical priesthood of Aaron (a father) and his four sons (sonship).

The pattern God intends for His Church and His people is to be established as a strong influential apostolic and prophetic New Testament Church; walking with the kingdom of God understanding and perspective - (pursuing God's priority - Matthew 6:10, 33); and being established as a family in the order of Father and sonship.

This is an Apostolic/Prophetic - Kingdom - Fathering/Sonship season.

What is missing in today's leadership and emerging Church is the establishment of true apostolic and prophetic fathers and sons who are pursuing God's priority - His kingdom. We are missing the apostolic foundation and therefore missing the apostolic pattern and the Due Order of God. The place of true Apostolic Fathers in today's Church and society cannot be overemphasized. This is a fatherless generation that is breaching the Spirit and releasing a curse. We have failed to see the important need for spiritual fathers and sonship principle and pattern the Lord has established in His family because we are blind to this eternal truth.

I believe as we give ourselves to seek His will, and make His kingdom our principal goal, then He can trust us with essential truths that are foundational to His purpose.

I remember presenting a New Testament principle to challenge leaders to re-examine their lives and to establish the right pattern of the Lord for the building of His house. The overseer stood up afterward to thank me for the ministry of the word and how timely it was for them to hear this, but he went on to say to his leaders that they do love other churches, but they are a 'denomination' and that 'denomination' they will be, and he went on further to encourage the leaders to build according to the pattern of the denomination. He missed the point! We are not talking about building according to the pattern of a denomination, or to a specific church fellowship. We are talking about building the Church of Jesus Christ according to His pattern. This requires that every denomination and Church fellowship must restructure to align to an authentic New Testament principle and pattern that the Lord has ordered, so the Lord will abide with His people, if not we will continue to build according to the traditions of men which is a hindrance to what the Lord desires. We must set the right structure within our lives for His glory to abide.

With leadership comes responsibility; and the time is now for us to live accountably to His pattern. We must build faithfully according to God's blue print (pattern).

Building According To The Divine Pattern 24

Building On The Foundation

"Establishing The House On The Foundation Of Eternal Principle & Truth"

"If the foundations be destroyed, what can the righteous do?"
(Psalm 11:3).

Chapter Two

Building On The Foundation

In this chapter, we are going to look into some foundational principles which are eternal truths and prerequisites for building the house of God (the Church) according to God's pattern.

We have established the fact that God is building His house, which is the Church; because He seeks to dwell among His people. The understanding is that it must be done according to His pattern.

If there is a building, there must be a foundation for the building.

The first order of eternal principle in the building of God's house - the Church, is to establish the right foundation that has been prescribed in God's divine pattern. To build the house of God for Him to dwell, we must learn the importance of a solid foundation which is the basis to building according to the pattern.

Once we have an accurate prophetic view and understanding of the blueprint of God's house we have to work out how to establish it in that order. Like someone said, it's a bit like coming up with a spectacular roof design for a skyscraper first, but to get it up there, you need to first build a solid foundation and support structures that are required.

Only to the extent that we desire and build according to the pattern can the Church fulfill the purpose of God and advance His kingdom. The Church will never reflect the intent and purpose of God, unless it is built upon the solid foundation of eternal principles.

One of the patterns God intends for His Church and His people is to be established as a strong influential apostolic and prophetic New Testament Church. The foundation of the New Testament Church is built upon the apostles and prophets, with Jesus Christ as the bedrock. This was, and is the pattern for every New Testament Church. The foundation of the apostles and prophets is the eternal prerequisite for building the Church of Jesus Christ according to the pattern.

"Built on the foundation of the apostles and prophets, Christ Jesus Himself being the cornerstone, in whom the whole structure, being joined together, grows into a holy temple in the Lord. In Him you also are being built together into a dwelling place for God by the Spirit" - (Ephesians 2:20-22 ESV).

A foundation is the solid base, which is an underlying basis or principle upon which something is built. The Church is built on the foundation of the apostles and prophets, and Jesus Christ Himself being the cornerstone.

This apostolic and prophetic foundation upon which the Church is built will determine the strength of the house and increase the stability of the structure. Upon this foundation the spiritual measurement of the structure and how far the Church can go towards perfection and maturity will be determined.

When the Church is accurately established upon the apostolic and prophetic grace, it then positions the people in their God given purpose in Christ as the body fits together and grows into a holy temple in the Lord (Ephesians 2:21).

The establishing of this foundational principle in the Church will also determine the spiritual destiny of the people, and provide a firm process for releasing spiritual growth and maturity into the stature of the fullness of Christ.

The Foundation Of The Apostles & Prophets:

The apostles and prophets are called foundational ministries because they lay the foundation for the building of the house of God. They are not the foundation; Jesus Christ is the foundation of the Church.

"You are built on the foundation of the apostles and prophets. Christ Jesus Himself is the cornerstone." - (Ephesians 2:20 GW).

The ministry of the apostles and prophets does not negate the ministry of the pastors, evangelists and teachers. They all compliment one another to fulfill the same purpose of equipping God's people, to serve and to build up the body of Christ until all of us are united in our faith and in our knowledge of God's Son, until we become mature and measure up to Christ, who is the standard (Ephesians 4:12-13).

However it is only to the apostles and prophets the Lord has given the grace to function as foundational ministry in the building of God's house - the Church. *This is God's pattern and anything outside this order is not a reflection of His will and pattern.*

Interestingly the New Testament Church in the book of Acts was predominantly the working of the apostles and prophets setting things in order. Nowhere do we hear of the term 'pastor' as a ***singular*** ministry, or see a pastoral pattern being established as the foundation or order of leadership in the Church. The New Testament churches in the book of Acts were all operating with an apostolic mindset as they built and established the Church in God's purpose and pattern.

The pastoral model being established as the foundation of the Church is an inaccurate pattern that continues to stand as an impediment against the apostolic and prophetic foundation. There is a need for us to make a transition in this season from this pattern and from the old pastoral leadership order, to build upon the foundation of the apostles and prophets and to have an apostolic leadership order of presbytery. We have to measure accurately the pattern and observe the whole form of its design, and make all things according to the pattern the Lord has given.

"Thou son of man, **shew the house to the house** of Israel, that they may be ashamed of their iniquities: and **let them measure the pattern**. And if they be ashamed of all that they have done, **shew them the form of the house, and the fashion thereof**, and the goings out thereof, and the comings in thereof, and all the forms thereof, and all the ordinances thereof… and all the laws thereof: and write it in their sight, **that they may keep the whole form thereof, and all the ordinances thereof, and do them**" - (Ezekiel 43:10-11).

When proper government of divine order is established within a local Church fellowship, the ministry continues to effectively function even after the death of the set-man, because the kingdom is not about us, it is about the KING. We have often seen the fall of many Church fellowships and organizations after the death of the set-man, because of the lack of true apostolic structure and presbytery of leadership. Things were built around the man, rather than on the foundation of the apostles and prophets. *Wrong pattern affects the continuity of the work.* We must change this old concept and begin to build generationally, and the only way to do that is to build according to the pattern God has revealed.

"Now if any man build upon this foundation gold, silver, precious stones, wood, hay, stubble; Every man's work shall be made manifest: for the day shall declare it, because it shall be revealed by fire; and the fire shall try every man's work of what sort it is. If any man's work abide which he hath built thereupon, he shall receive a reward. If any man's work shall be burned, he shall suffer loss: but he himself shall be saved; yet so as by fire. Know ye not that ye are the temple of God, and that the Spirit of God dwelleth in you?" - (1 Corinthians 3:12-16).

It is important to note here that the "apostolic and prophetic foundation" is not a program, or Church Growth strategy to increase membership, or a set of doctrines taught by apostles and prophets, but it is the impartation of the divine life of the Lord Jesus Christ that is established in us as the foundation, which is released through a unique relationship the ministry births us into with the Lord. It is an encounter with Christ who brings us into a certain quality of a unique relationship with God the Father.

The apostolic and prophetic is the grace of the Lord Jesus Christ that is bestowed in *a sent man,* who carries and expresses the divine nature of Christ to build the Church according to the pattern. The apostolic and prophetic ministries are not entertainers, they are foundational builders. This is what we must understand as we seek to transition our churches from a pastoral model to an apostolic and prophetic New Testament Church pattern that the Lord has ordained. This transition will release a new flow of the life of Christ in the Church beyond our present understanding and realm.

We are not an apostolic and prophetic Church because we have attended or hosted an apostolic conference or read some apostolic books that teach about the apostolic reformation. The primary means and instrument for transitioning a Church from the old order of things to an apostolic Church, is through an apostle and a prophet that the Lord has assigned for that purpose. It does not come through conferences or teaching notes. *We are an apostolic Church by relationship with "a sent one", and by the impartation and establishment of the divine order of Christ in us.* Through relationship there is an impartation of some spiritual gift (divine nature of Christ) that establishes an apostolic foundation in us.

"For I long to see you, that I may impart unto you some spiritual gift, to the end ye may be established" - (Romans 1:11).

This is where many are failing in the process of apostolic transition. Going to apostolic and prophetic meetings occasionally is not enough. *The apostolic is an encounter with a man the Lord yokes us with, who has the grace to bring us into this unique relationship with the divine nature of Christ.* This is not about the person that led you to the Lord for your salvation, but it is a spiritual experience and walk into the deeper life of Christ which is foundational to the purposes of God for His Church.

The apostolic and prophetic ministry carries a specific mandate to birth and establish things. It all depends on where you are in your walk in life and the ministry.

Firstly, there are those who already know who they are, that they are called into the apostolic and prophetic ministry and they are walking in this order, *but not accurately*. A matured and established apostle and prophet has the grace to help establish such a person and ministry in this order so things can be built *more* accurately according to the pattern.

Secondly, there are those who must be completely birthed into this new walk and dimension in their life and ministry. They need to completely shift from the old ways to a new way in Christ in order to be preserved in this new season. It is a complete renewal of the wineskin, because new wine cannot be placed in old wineskin - Matthew 9:17.

An example of this transition is seen with Apollos receiving impartation from Aquila and Priscilla to help him walk accurately in the way of God - Acts 18:24-28. This is only possible where there is a true expression of humility and relationship.

There must be an ever-flowing revelation of present truth through a "sent one" who is a true apostle of the Lord Jesus Christ that God sets over a man and his local house (Church fellowship) as a conduit, through an established covenant relationship. When we lack relationship with an apostolic and prophetic ministry that God sets over us, we become like a parched land.

It is therefore imperative that we prayerfully reconsider some of our relationships and make a transition into a covenant relationship with the *sent one* God has preordained for us. This is in no wise requesting that you break existing relationships in an ungodly manner and cause division and bad feeling; but this is to align you to the right ministry grace and order the Father has purposed. This is about your destiny! Being a part of an ongoing relationship that you are submitting to that is not fulfilling this purpose is not a life sentence. God is breaking off old relationships that have not served His purpose to impart the divine life of Christ in us nor produced the pattern and the purposes of God in carrying us further in God. We are being released into divine relationships which is characterized by apostolic and prophetic grace to help establish this eternal foundation and pattern for the Church.

Every local Church fellowship must have a functioning and an established relationship with the five fold ministry gifts of the apostle, prophet, evangelist, pastor and teacher to fulfill God's purpose for the Church.

"And He gave some, apostles; and some, prophets; and some, evangelists; and some, pastors and teachers; For the perfecting of the saints, for the work of the ministry, for the edifying of the body of Christ: Till we all come in the unity of the faith, and of the knowledge of the Son of God, unto a perfect man, unto the measure of the stature of the fullness of Christ: That we henceforth be no more children, tossed to and fro, and carried about with every wind of doctrine, by the sleight of men, and cunning craftiness, whereby they lie in wait to deceive; But speaking the truth in love, may grow up into Him in all things, which is the head, even Christ: From whom the whole body fitly joined together and compacted by that which every joint supplieth, according to the effectual working in the measure of every part, maketh increase of the body unto the edifying of itself in love" - (Ephesians 4:11-16).

We are focusing only on the foundational ministry of the apostle and prophet in this book. Like we said, this does not negate the ministry of the evangelist, pastor and teacher, because they are all important and needed for the building of God's house. The evangelists, pastors and teachers are well known and received within the spiritual circle of the Body, but the foundational ministry of the apostle and prophet are not well received because of unbiblical perception, wrong mindset about these ministry gifts, and the misinterpretation of the gifts and pattern of God for the Church.

The Foundational Doctrines of Christ:

Now that we are saved, what next?

The challenge facing the Church is the lack of understanding and direction of God's purpose for us. Many are enslaved by the mentality that they were only saved for heaven. As a result of this they are idle and waiting for death or a sudden intrusion.

Now that we are saved, the first step is to be established on the foundational doctrine of Christ.

"Therefore leaving the principles of the doctrine of Christ, let us go on unto perfection; not laying again the foundation of repentance from dead works, and of faith toward God, Of the doctrine of baptisms, and of laying on of hands, and of resurrection of the dead, and of eternal judgment. And this will we do, if God permit" - (Hebrews 6:1-3).

The inevitable peril of immaturity and falling away is certain when we camp around the principles of the doctrines of Christ, which are considered to be elementary, without advancing towards maturity (growing up in Christ) and to move on to the deeper things of God.

Nonetheless, we cannot talk about moving on to perfection, maturity or growing up in Christ and in the deeper things of God, without first being established in the basic foundational truths which are considered to be the fundamental doctrines of Christ, and also the true doctrinal foundation of the apostles and prophets.

The Church's belief system must be based on the foundation of Hebrews 6:1-2, and not our own interpretation of it, but comparing spiritual (the Word) with spiritual (the Word).

There are six foundational doctrines of Christ listed in Hebrews 6:1-2.

1. *Repentance from dead works*
2. *Faith toward God*
3. *The doctrine of baptisms*
4. *Laying on of hands*
5. *Resurrection of the dead*
6. *Eternal judgment*

Building On The Foundation 36

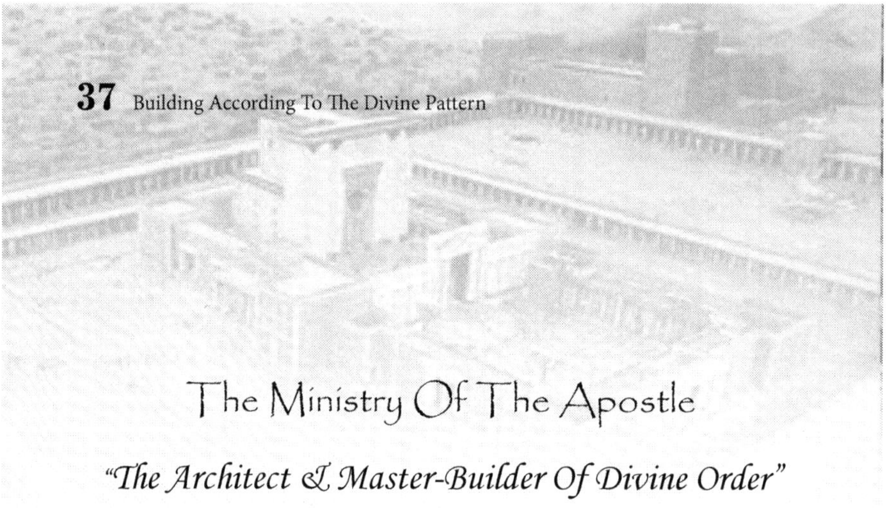

The Ministry Of The Apostle

"The Architect & Master-Builder Of Divine Order"

"According to the grace of God which is given unto me, as a wise masterbuilder, I have laid the foundation, and another buildeth thereon. But let every man take heed how he buildeth thereupon. For other foundation can no man lay than that is laid, which is Jesus Christ"
(1 Corinthians 3:10-11).

Chapter Three

The Ministry Of The Apostle

As we seek to build accurately on the foundation of the apostles and prophets (Ephesians 2:20), it is imperative for us to know and understand the ministry of the apostle and the prophet, because they are foundational ministries.

Who Is An Apostle?

The term "apostle" comes from a Greek word ***"apostolos"***, which is translated to be a 'sent one', a delegate; specifically an ambassador of the Gospel assigned on a specific mission to represent the interests of the kingdom of God. This is God's *messenger*, who walks in authority and miraculous powers while representing the name of the sender - Jesus Christ. They are sent with a specific call by the Lord. In the New Testament, this word "apostles" describes those sent out by the Lord to preach the gospel of the kingdom - Matthew 10:1-7. They are a kingdom herald.

There are different kind of apostles revealed in scripture:

The Apostles of the Lamb – These were the twelve men the Lord Jesus selected to carry out the work of the gospel with Him - Mark 3:13-19. There will not be any more of these. They are unique and were appointed during the earthly ministry of Jesus. They are the eternal foundation ministry of the Church, and the *only* 'apostles of the Lamb'.

"And the wall of the city had twelve foundations, and in them the names of the twelve apostles of the Lamb." - (Revelation 21:14).

The Ascension Apostles – These apostles were appointed after the ascension of the Lord Jesus to heaven, and they continue to function to this day. The Lord is still appointing them. Apart from the twelve apostles of the Lamb, all apostles mentioned now and in scripture are ascension apostles.

a. Paul (Ephesians 1:1).
b. Barnabas (Acts 14:14).
c. Epaphroditus (Philippians 2:25).
d. Andronicus and Junius (Romans 16:7).
e. Others were noted by association such as Timothy and Titus.

"Whether any do inquire of Titus, he is my partner and fellowhelper concerning you: or our brethren be inquired of, they are the *messengers* [word used in the Greek is *"apostolos"*] of the churches, and the glory of Christ." - (2 Corinthians 8:23 brackets mine).

The apostle is a measure of the grace of the Lord Jesus Christ that is given to the Church as a ministry gift. It is not the fullness in itself, but it is a measure of grace that is given by the Lord Jesus to serve a specific purpose in the Church.

"But unto every one of us is given grace according to the measure of the gift of Christ" - (Ephesians 4:7).

Every believer has a measure of an apostolic grace and commission on their life, but this does not make everyone an apostle. Jesus declared, **"As the Father has sent (apostello) me, so I send you" - (John 20:21)**. This makes every believer apostolic in nature, but not in calling.

How To Know And Identify An Apostle:

First and foremost, an apostle is a custodian of the mysteries of Christ, and the revelation of the purposes of God. They are characterized and known by the revelation of God's kingdom, and the mysteries (present truth) of Christ that they receive and bring forth into the body of Christ. This is a unique mark among others that clearly defines an apostle.

"Let a man so account of us (apostles), as of the ministers of Christ, and stewards of the mysteries of God" - (1 Corinthians 4:1).

"If ye have heard of the dispensation of the grace of God which is given me to you-ward: How that *by revelation He made known unto me the mystery;* (as I wrote afore in few words, Whereby, when ye read, ye may understand my knowledge in the mystery of Christ). *Which in other ages was not made known unto the sons of men, as it is now revealed unto His holy apostles and prophets by the Spirit*" - (Ephesians 3:2-5).

All other ministry gifts like the Pastor, Evangelist and the Teacher have a measure of revelation in them that they impart to the body, but there are certain revelations of the mysteries of Christ which are foundational, and it is *only* given to the apostles and prophets by the Holy Spirit to impart to the Church.

The apostolic calling is not in the clerical collar or the ecclesiastical robes that is worn. These are just religious garments and it does not count in this season. What counts is the grace that is given by the Lord Jesus Christ to fulfill a specific purpose in His plan for His Church.

In my study of other materials, most writers/theologians have laid down certain criteria from the ministry of Paul the apostle as the four primary conditions for one to be called an apostle, which we will briefly look at. These conditions are part of the work and experience of an apostle, but they do not necessarily make you an apostle.

1. He must have planted churches - 1 Corinthians 9:1-2.

Planting of churches is one of the apostolic assignments of an apostle, but this does not make anyone an apostle. The error we find among leaders is the wrong teachings and the idea that because of the number of churches they have planted they have now ascended into the office of an apostle. In other words; everyone who has planted churches is now seen as an apostle. However somebody may show up in any part of the world with enough financial resources and recruit leaders and plant ten churches or more in one day, but this doesn't make them an apostle. The apostolic ministry is not merited by works or by the planting of churches.

2. He must have seen the Lord - 1 Corinthians 9:1.

Paul the apostle defended his own apostolic ministry as one who had seen the Lord like the other apostles of the Lamb. However, there is no scriptural evidence to prove that to be an apostle you must see the Lord, neither did the following apostles who were commissioned for ministry by the Church saw the Lord personally: Barnabas (Acts 14:14), Apollos (1 Corinthians 4:6, 9), Silas and Timothy (1 Thessalonians 1:1, 2:6), Sosthenes (1 Corinthians 1:1), and others.

As a leader, if seeing the Lord in a vision qualifies you to be an apostle as Paul the apostle did, then there will be several leaders today who are not called to be apostles, but they have seen the Lord, and continue to see the Lord in visions.

It is a privilege to see Jesus Christ our Lord, just as some of the apostles did, but this is not what makes one an apostle.

3. He must have suffered for the faith - 1 Corinthians 4:9-13.

The early apostles and disciples suffered much for their faith in Christ as they went about proclaiming the gospel of the kingdom. They were often ostracized by their own families and communities. Some of the worst persecution came from the religious leaders (Acts 4:1–3). As in the early church times, many believers today have found that making a public proclamation of faith in Christ can result in imprisonment, beatings, torture, and death (Hebrews 11:32–38; 2 Corinthians 12:10; Philippians 3:8; Acts 5:40).

We have not only been given the privilege of trusting in Christ, but also the privilege of **suffering** for Him. Jesus said, "Blessed are those who are persecuted because of righteousness, for theirs is the kingdom of heaven" (Matthew 5:10).

"Everyone who wants to live a godly life in Christ Jesus will be persecuted." - (2 Timothy 3:12 NIV).

Apostles will suffer and be ostracized for their faith in Christ, but suffering is not a criterion to qualify one as an apostle, because every disciple that will live for Christ will suffer for Christ. This therefore is not a yardstick to measure an apostle.

4. He must have signs of powers and miracles.

"While I was among you I patiently did the signs, wonders, and miracles which prove that I'm an apostle" - (2 Corinthians 12:12).

I strongly believe every true apostolic ministry will be characterized by signs and mighty works as a proof of the apostolic ministry. This in many ways will reveal Christ and draw people into the kingdom.

No man is qualified into this office by his experience or by his accomplished works to become an apostle or part of the five fold ministry. Every apostleship is a predestined call in Christ that a man has been preordained to walk in before the foundation of the world. His spiritual experience is therefore the result of this prophetic destiny, and his accomplished works are the after-products or fruits of his apostolic function.

It is not something that is earned or qualified for by works or experience. Don't be beguiled by spiritual experience and accomplished works to think that they have caused you to ascend to become an apostle or any other gift ministry. *If heaven has not called and endorsed you into the office of an apostle or any ministry gifts, your experience and your accomplished works will not make you one.*

Critical examination of the twelve apostles of the Lamb and other apostles mentioned in the scriptures such as Paul, will prove that none of them were called into their apostleship because of their spiritual experience or works accomplished, but rather, it was a response to the heavenly call that gave them an experi ence, and brought them into a spiritual journey in order to have that divine encounter with Christ, which gave them knowledge of their apostolic call and assignment.

True apostles and prophets do not operate from their title, but from their relationship with the sender - Jesus Christ.

"And God hath set some in the church, *first* apostles, secondarily prophets, thirdly teachers, after that miracles, then gifts of healings, helps, governments, diversities of tongues" - (1 Corinthians 12:28).

As we have earlier stated, apostles and prophets are foundational builders. They are *first* because the foundation of the Church is built by them. The building of a house requires that those who lay the foundation should be the *first* to begin the work. This does not make them more important or superior than the other builders, but their job description requires that they be the first to serve (work).

"For I think that God has set forth us the apostles *last*, as it were appointed to death: for we are made a spectacle unto the world, and to angels, and to men" - (1 Corinthians 4:9).

How can apostles be both first and last?

In truth, the ministry of an apostle is not a ministry gift to be elevated above others, as some presume. The apostle or the apostolic is not about position, but speaks of a function and an order of pioneering in the building process of the house of God. The apostolic is the function of the gift of the grace of Jesus Christ to the Body for service. ***They are servant ministry, and not master ministry***.

If the apostle or the apostolic does not function as a service (servant ministry) to the Body then it is not the pattern that the Lord has ordained for the Church.

The emphasis on offices, positions, ranks and titles is affecting the development and the restoration of the true intent of God for these ministry gifts within the Church. The mindset of apostolic ranking and governmental positions to rule and control the people of God is a manipulation of God's Church, and this is birthed out of the religious system of babylon which is not the order of God. Any assembly or ministry office that is established and operating in this pattern is not building according to the pattern of God.

We have only redressed the institutional church structures and denominational positions to a new terminology and ranking, but the pattern continues to be the same old wineskin, hence we are not advancing beyond the old order. We therefore need to pull down this hierarchy structure and pyramid type of ministry and establish a true apostolic servant ministry that reflects a New Testament presbytery. This transition of ministry is necessary for the Church in order for it to be built according to the pattern of God.

I have often said that if the present process of reformation is causing us to walk in pride and arrogance because of our new titles (as apostle, prophet, bishops etc), or if it is not bringing the people of God to the place of obedience to God's will and way, then something is wrong with that system and pattern we are operating in.

There has to be a clear revelation of this foundational principle to help us see the big picture of the way God has set things.

This will help us to remain humble as servant ministry, rather than our fleshy pursuit for titles, authority and control over the Church.

Humility is one of the characters of an apostle. Humility is the solid foundation of all moral standards, and every true apostle must possess this particular moral excellence.

"And there is not a created thing not manifest before Him, but all things are naked and open to His eyes—with whom is our reckoning" - (Hebrews 4:13 YLT).

Those who live in the light (revelation) cannot be proud, because they know they are naked before Him. It is only while dwelling in darkness (ignorance) that we can be full of pride and seek for positions of ranking in order to control and manipulate.

One of the greatest revelation you can have is the discovery of yourself. Self discovery will help us see the way God sees us and will cause us to prostrate and overcome our flesh, arrogance and pride, knowing that all things are naked and exposed before Him whom we must give account to. Revelation enables us to see the way God sees things.

"Through whom (Christ) we have received grace and apostleship to bring about the obedience of faith for the sake of His name among all the nations" - (Romans 1:5 emphasis is mine).

One of the purposes for the ministry of apostleship is to release a certain measure of grace for the obedience to the faith among all nations.

To walk in a true apostolic way will require obedience that will bring death to our flesh and every human desire, way, method and doctrine in order to embrace a higher life and order of the divine nature of Christ.

There is no faith without obedience, and true obedience will bring humility and death that will release us into the purposes of God.

Jesus is our pattern and Chief Apostle by whom we must model our life and ministry; Therefore this must be a watchword for us - *"And being found in fashion as a man, He (Jesus) humbled Himself, and became obedient unto death, even the death of the cross" - (Philippians 2:8).*

Any faith you cannot die for is not worth believing.

"We are persecuted, but God does not leave us. We are hurt sometimes, but we are not destroyed. We carry the death of Jesus in our own bodies so that the life of Jesus can also be seen in our bodies. We are alive, but for Jesus we are always in danger of death so that the life of Jesus can be seen in our bodies that die." - (2 Corinthians 4:9-11 New Century Version).

"When I was with you, I was patient...." - (2 Corinthians 12:12a CEV).

The lifestyle of a true apostle is not only proven by miracles and powerful actions, but also in his humility, patience and sufferings. These are part of the experience with Christ, but the joy is, if we suffer with Him, we will also be glorified together. For the sufferings of this present time are not worthy to be compared with the glory which shall be revealed in us - Romans 8:17-18.

Patience is one of the hallmarks of a true apostle. This character is an inward quality that is tested in the furnace of trials and persecution. It is important to note that as an apostle one is bound to face much persecution and suffering. Great perseverance determines an apostle's authenticity.

Another important aspect of the ministry of the apostle is the anguish they go through to impart Christ to the Body and establishing them in the measure of the stature of the fullness of Christ.

"My little children, of whom I travail in birth again until Christ be formed in you" - (Galatians 4:19).

One of the qualities of the apostle is the ability to walk in wisdom as a kingdom builder (wise master-builder). It takes wisdom to build accurately.

"According to the grace of God which is given unto me, as a wise master-builder...." - (1 Corinthians 3:10).

An apostle brings order to the Church and corrects problems. An apostle does not leave things as they are, but sets things in order and ordains leadership. The absence of real order in the Church today is traceable to the lack of apostolic presence and apostolic authority. One of the reasons we need apostles is because the Church is out of order, and the apostolic ministry is mandated to set things in order.

"For this cause left I thee in Crete, that thou shouldest set in order the things that are wanting, and ordain elders in every city, as I had appointed thee:" - (Titus 1:5).

An apostle imparts gifts and strengthens the Churches. Apostles strengthen Churches just as the natural father strengthens the family. This ministry benefits every disciple and the Church at-large.

"And he went through Syria and Cilicia, confirming the churches." - (Acts 15:41).

In the Greek the word "confirming" is translated **"episterizo"**, which means to strengthen or re-establish.

"For I long to see you, that I may impart unto you some spiritual gift, to the end ye may be established;" - (Romans 1:11).

The apostle strives to preach the gospel of the kingdom where Christ is not known, and to establish New Testament based churches (Romans 15:20; 2 Corinthians 10:16). The heart of an apostle is for the "regions beyond". They operate with a geographical mindset in alignment with their specific calling.

Every apostle must know their metron.

The apostolic ministry is relationally-based, which is clearly seen in his unrestricted love for the Church. The apostle is not autocratic, demanding, but relational and supportive (1 Thessalonians 2:6; 2 Corinthians 1:24). They have a passionate love and care for the Church. The present state of the Church compels true apostles to seek God's will and intent for the Church. Their heart is a heart of love and a desire for the Church to mature.

Genuine love for the Church will not allow the apostle (apostolic) to live an irresponsible lifestyle that fleeces the Body, or to merchandise the gifts (grace of Christ) for a price tag that robs and exploit the churches.

"Beside those things that are without, that which cometh upon me daily, the care of all the churches." - (2 Corinthians 11:28).

The strength and ministry growth of true apostolic ministry is measured by Christ's stature that is imparted and established in the Body, and not by monuments of buildings, membership, financial status or the number of countries traveled to (2 Corinthians 10: 12-15).

Suggested Reading:
Apostolic Strategies for Kingdom Reformation - Series 2
(The Apostolic Ministry & The Work)
Author: Israel Onoriobe

The Ministry Of The Prophet

"The Trumpetic Voice Of God Declaring His Purposes Unveiling the Blueprint"

"Shall a trumpet be blown in the city, and the people not be afraid? shall there be evil in a city, and the LORD hath not done it? **Surely the Lord GOD will do nothing, but He revealeth His secret unto His servants the prophets**" (Amos 3:6-7).

Chapter Four

The Ministry Of The Prophet

As we explore the ministry of the prophet as a foundational ministry in building the Church according to the pattern, I have taken this as an excerpt from my book, "Apostolic Strategies for Kingdom Reformation - Series 2", under the subheading "Apostolic Impartation & Character", and I have expanded more on it to help us further understand this ministry gift.

Who Is A Prophet?

The Hebrew word for "prophet" is **"nabiy"**; one who prophesy through the inspiration of the Holy Spirit. To prophesy is to reveal, predict the future, and speak the mind of God for the purpose of direction, building and encouragement to the Church.

"Beforetime in Israel, when a man went to inquire of God, thus he spake, Come, and let us go to the seer: for he that is now called a Prophet was beforetime called a Seer." - (1 Samuel 9:9).

"Seer" comes from the Hebrew word *"ra'ah"* which means one who has the ability to see or perceive. It also denotes one who is a beholder of visions.

In Greek, the word "prophet" means *"prophetis"*, a foreteller or an inspired speaker. It is important to note here that the same Greek word used for a prophet is the same Greek word used for a prophetess. They are foreteller or an inspired speaker. A prophetess is not the wife of a prophet, but a foreteller or an inspired woman speaker with the same grace as a prophet. This grace of God and its function to the Body is not limited to men, but it is also for women. <u>God is not gender bias</u>.

A prophet is a gift that is given by the Lord Jesus to His Church (Ephesians 4:8-11). They are first and foremost a foundational ministry to the Body with a primary mandate to equip the saints to do the work of the ministry, to grow in unity, into maturity and Christ-likeness.

Prophets are key players in the program of God for the building of His Church, and for His purpose on earth. They are instrumental in revealing the secret and plans of God to us. They receive direct revelation from God which they reveal and impart to the Church.

"Surely the Lord GOD will do nothing, but He revealeth His secret unto His servants the prophets" - (Amos 3:7).

The ministry of the prophet is a type of a trumpet that gives a distinct sound and voice from heaven to announce and declare God's purpose in the earth. They are sometimes misunderstood because of the uniqueness of their assignment and voice - Numbers 10:1-10.

Prophets operate frequently in the spiritual 'gift of prophecy' and 'word of knowledge'. However, the "Gift of a Prophet" is different from the "Gift of Prophecy" and "Word of Knowledge.

It is important for us to note here that the "Gift of Prophecy" and "Word of Knowledge" are motivational gifts which is part of the nine spiritual gifts of the Holy Spirit which is freely given to the Body of Christ, and they can be manifested by any disciple of Christ filled with the Holy Spirit according to 1 Corinthians 12: 8-10. But this does not make every disciple who operates in the gifts of "Word of Knowledge' and "Prophecy" to be a prophet.

(A) The 'Gift of Prophecy' is the ability to motivate people through the proclamation of the word of God (telling forth the Word of God) so that each believer can profit for the common good of serving others as lives are changed, but the 'Gift of a Prophet' has much to do with *prediction* as with *proclamation*. This therefore allows the prophet to be able to review the past and accurately predict the upcoming (share a word about the future), but fundamentally sheds light on the present. A prophet is able to predict, to sense and become aware of things that are future.

(B) The gift of 'Word of Knowledge' is the divine ability to have knowledge of a thing and to reveal a matter by the inspiration of the Holy Spirit without reliance on human knowledge which now allows for the application of wisdom in that matter to bring counsel and direction so everyone can profit withal. This gift allows the disciple to have knowledge of what is happening.

The 'Gift of a Prophet' is in a different impartation and order of the administration of the grace of Christ that is ministered to the Church that makes them foundational, and they can also function as a governmental office in the Church. This ministry grace far exceeds the ability to motivate and to have knowledge of things.

The prophetic ministry is more than just calling names and revealing things to amuse and charm people. The prophetic ministry must function primarily to activate Christ in the people, and to impart His nature in the Church in order to release the saints into their prophetic destiny to hear the voice of God for themselves and to respond to Him accordingly.

In this season of restoration, we must know the voice of God, or we will miss God and what He is doing. In the restoration of all things, change is constant and this depends on our obedience to His speaking voice. The Church must be able to accurately discern the voice of God, and to know what God is doing in this present season. Our ability to clearly hear and know the voice of God will determine the process of our place and position in God. This is where the prophetic ministry is needful.

Unfortunately, some only desire the ministry of the prophet for a personal word of prophecy to meet their needs rather than developing their own ability to hear and respond to the way of God. They want the prophet to tell them about their past, present and future. We need to recognize that the prophet is more that just a medium of knowledge for our past and future; they are not psychic or entertainers, but they are a foundational gift that brings a certain level of establishment and maturity in Christ to the Church. If Christ is not established and seen in the people through the prophetic ministry to them, then such prophetic ministries are questionable in their acts.

We must be very careful and discern every prophetic ministry, because ignorance of the true ministry of the prophet, and the desperate need for prophecy among the people has given room to the demonic spirit of divination, which is known as a python spirit that now operates in some churches today. This false prophetic ministry is called a "python spirit" which is derived from the Greek word ***"pytho"***, meaning an office of the Delphic oracle, a priestess of the ancient Greek god called Apollo who had a spirit of divination - the art of obtaining secret knowledge (of people and events), which is the counterfeit of the prophetic Spirit and the word of knowledge.

"And it came to pass, as we went to prayer, a certain damsel possessed with a spirit of divination (***Greek: "pytho" - python spirit***) met us, which brought her masters much gain by soothsaying: The same followed Paul and us, and cried, saying, These men are the servants of the most high God, which shew unto us the way of salvation. And this did she many days. But Paul, being grieved, turned and said to the spirit, I command thee in the name of Jesus Christ to come out of her. And he came out the same hour" - (Acts 16:16-18 Emphasis is mine).

A python is a non-poisonous constricting snake that has the power to squeeze its prey to death. This demonic spirit seeks to squeeze the life of God from the Church. This ancient demonic spirit is manifesting in the church today, and trying to squash the life of God from the Church. This python spirit causes distraction which affects the pattern of God. It tends to kill the operation of the Spirit of God in the prayer and worship of God's people.

"Beware of false prophets, which come to you in sheep's clothing, but inwardly they are ravening wolves. Ye shall know them by their fruits...." - (Matthew 7:15-16).

"Beloved, believe not every spirit, but try the spirits whether they are of God: because many false prophets are gone out into the world" - (1 John 4:1).

There are many false prophets out there who are cunning and full of deviousness. We must be very discerning to know these false spirits among us. Their fruits will expose them. The truth will always expose the deception and fakes, and bring divine order and restoration. It takes the grace of God to accomplish this and to bear witness of the truth.

We need to identify and recognize true prophets and begin to give them room to operate along with the other five-fold ministry gifts. If the Church is to come into maturity in Christ, then we must recognize the existence of the office and ministry of the prophets in the Body of Christ, and receive them in the order the Lord has given this gift to the Church.

The prophet serves as God's representative that is close to the heart of God and speaks God's mind and purpose to His people. They reveal the mind of God to the people through the inspiration of the Holy Spirit. They also bring divine guidance and direction because they can foresee the future and as well predict accurately the things the Lord has ordained.

"And in these days came prophets from Jerusalem unto Antioch. And there stood up one of them named Agabus, and signified by the Spirit that there should be great dearth throughout all the world: which came to pass in the days of Claudius Caesar. Then the disciples, every man according to his ability, determined to send relief unto the brethren which dwelt in Judaea: Which also they did, and sent it to the elders by the hands of Barnabas and Saul" - (Acts 11:27-30).

Part of the prophetic function is to "exhort" and "confirm" the Church.

"And Judas and Silas, being prophets also themselves, exhorted the brethren with many words, and confirmed them." - (Acts 15:32).

To exhort means to encourage. In the Greek the word is ***"parakaleo"*** which describes the prophetic function as "to call near, invite, invoke (by imploration or consolation), call for, or to entreat".

To 'confirm' comes from the Greek word "**episterizo**", which means "to support further, re-establish or strengthen". This is also a prophetic function in the Church.

It is wise to commend and honour the prophets that have carried the Church through past prophetic seasons by the grace of God. True prophets have stood the test of time and declared this present season in the midst of rejection. The prophetic ministry is a ministry of rejection. Many will reject and condemn the prophets because of God's revealed truth - the truth of God's word that is revealed to them in bringing correction and alignment.

I had an experience while ministering on one of my mission trips overseas and laying this foundational principle. The Lord gave me a prophetic word concerning a person in the congregation to pray against an attack of the enemy coming against the family and to alert them to watch in prayers, and to also call for accurate alignment with the Lord. The person rejected the prophetic word and made a public ridicule of the teachings that I had given, saying it was all cooked up and delivered to me by the leadership of the church, because without any prior knowledge I had touched on some sensitive issues that were going on, and my word had brought counsel and order to the people. Wow! It was a shocking experience, but to God be the glory, the word of the Lord prevailed and the will of God was established in that congregation.

The prophetic ministry aligns the Church with God's purpose. It will expose sin, bring correction and order to the Body. The prophetic ministry will reveal the righteous judgment of God.

A true prophet does not compromise the revelation of God to His people. His nature must always demand that action be taken - something must be done.

True matured prophetic ministry does not bring condemnation to the Body of Christ, but it brings encouragement. Though it will expose sin, but not primarily to make a mockery of the Church and bring punishment on the people, (though God will punish the people if they do not respond and repent to His prophetic word). The prophetic ministry is focused on revealing the truth in order to restore fellowship back with God. This is how maturity is displayed in the prophetic ministry.

"Therefore thus saith the Lord GOD, Behold, I lay in Zion for a foundation a stone, a tried stone, a precious corner stone, a sure foundation: he that believeth shall not make haste. Judgment also will I lay to the line, and righteousness to the plummet: and the hail shall sweep away the refuge of lies, and the waters shall overflow the hiding place." (Isaiah 28:16-17).

Though the prophets are sometimes considered to be harsh because of their approach to expose and rebuke sin, but it is a compassionate ministry that operates on the platform of love. The absence of love in the prophetic ministry will result in abuse and insult - (speaking to or treating the people with disrespect or scornful abuse). We must be very careful that we do not use the gifts to abuse the very Bride of Christ; otherwise, the bridegroom (Christ) will bring retribution.

A true prophetic ministry will reveal Christ and lead others to Him, and not draw men to themselves. The ministry is not self-driven to draw attention to itself because of its ability to see, hear and reveal things. The prophetic ministry must always be a sign-post pointing to Christ.

"The next day John seeth Jesus coming unto him, and saith, Behold the Lamb of God, which taketh away the sin of the world. This is He of whom I said, After me cometh a man which is preferred before me: for He was before me. And I knew Him not: but that He should be made manifest to Israel, therefore am I come baptizing with water. And John bare record, saying, I saw the Spirit descending from heaven like a dove, and it abode upon Him. And I knew Him not: but He that sent me to baptize with water, the same said unto me, Upon whom thou shalt see the Spirit descending, and remaining on Him, the same is He which baptizeth with the Holy Ghost. And I saw, and bare record that this is the Son of God. Again the next day after John stood, and two of his disciples; And looking upon Jesus as He walked, he saith, Behold the Lamb of God! And the two disciples heard him speak, and they followed Jesus." (John 1:29-37).

Many are drawn to the ministry of the prophet, but the purpose of the prophetic ministry is to draw people to God. The ministry of the prophet is a conduit between God and His Church.

The function of the prophetic ministry in the local assembly is supported by the operation of the other ministry gifts, as all is needed to equally impart their grace. ***The prophet works closely with the apostle as a team builder to lay foundation and bring strength and order to the Body of Christ. The prophet has the ability to see the blue print of the building of the house, while the apostle as a wise master-builder is able to take the blue print as revealed by the prophet and establish the order as shown by the Lord (1 Corinthians 3:9-11)***. God has given His grace to apostles and prophets to receive a revelation of His mysteries and to reveal them to the Body **(Ephesians 3:1-7)**.

This makes both ministries foundational builders with an identical function to the Body.

The foundational ministry of the apostles and prophets is not *optional*, but it is an essential and indispensable ministry that is needed and required to build the Church accurately according to the pattern. They are unique and distinctive ministries which are requisite and central in this present season to establish the Church, along with the other ministry gifts of Evangelist, Pastor and Teacher.

"All you inhabitants of the world, you who dwell on the earth, when a signal is raised on the mountains, look! When a trumpet is blown, hear!" - (Isaiah 18:3).

There is a *new sound* of the prophetic voice and ministry upon the earth today. It is my prayers and desire that we as a Church will gravitate towards this prophetic voice of God.

Suggested Reading:
Apostolic Strategies for Kingdom Reformation - Series 2
(The Apostolic Ministry & The Work)
Author: Israel Onoriobe

The Ever-Widening Kingdom

"Then said he, Unto what is the kingdom of God like? and whereunto shall I resemble it? It is like a grain of mustard seed, which a man took, and cast into his garden; and it grew, and waxed a great tree; and the fowls of the air lodged in the branches of it. And again he said, Whereunto shall I liken the kingdom of God? It is like leaven, which a woman took and hid in three measures of meal, till the whole was leavened." - (Luke 13:18-21).

The kingdom of God is a present reality that is active on earth now, and it is expanding. The kingdom of God is within us through the indwelling of the Holy Spirit in us. However, there are some aspects of God's kingdom that are future reality, which will only manifest at the fullness of age - at Christ appearing.

"And when He was demanded of the Pharisees, when the kingdom of God should come, He answered them and said, The kingdom of God cometh not with observation: Neither shall they say, Lo here! or, lo there! for, behold, the kingdom of God is within you"
(Luke 17:20-21).

We continue to press-on in the Kingdom, and contend for the faith by the grace of God, as we await the fullness and consummation of all things in Christ.

Chapter Five

The Ever-Widening Kingdom

We cannot build according to the divine pattern of God's concept without a clear revelation and understanding of the kingdom, because the whole of God's purpose is centered on His kingdom, which He has kept and concealed in Christ Jesus before the foundation of the world.

It is therefore fundamental to know the basics of God's purpose. God's will is for His kingdom (His Government, Rule, Reign and Dominion) to be established on earth as it is in heaven - to bring all things on earth under dominion in Christ Jesus.

"Let your kingdom come. Let your will be done on earth as it is done in heaven" - (Matthew 6:10 GW).

"When He (God) revealed the mystery of His plan to us. He had decided to do this through Christ. He planned to bring all of history to its goal in Christ. Then Christ would be the head of everything in heaven and on earth" - (Ephesians 1:9-10 GW).

This is the goal and master-plan of God's idea for the earth, and we cannot afford to misconstrue Him and His purpose. Every other thing is tangential and they all work in proportion to fulfill this goal.

This is the sole reason we have been chosen and apprehended by Christ Jesus. God has revealed and made Himself known to us through Christ, so that we might know Him, and the justification of this revelation in the knowledge of Him is to be conformed to this plan.

Every fiber of our being, our thoughts and our actions must be in pursuit of this master-plan of God's idea for the earth. Our day-to-day living, our marriage, our family, our work, our career and all of our ambitions must focus to equate His purpose, which is His kingdom for which we have been laid hold of by Christ Jesus. This is the purpose for our salvation, and our reason for life on earth.

Our salvation is because of His kingdom. We are saved for His kingdom.

"I pray that you will be grateful to God for letting you have part in what He has promised His people in the kingdom of light. God rescued us from the dark power of Satan and brought us into the kingdom of His dear Son" - (Colossians 1:12-13).

Heaven is not the origin of the Kingdom. God is the origin of the Kingdom. It comes from God. Without God there is no Kingdom and heaven is nothing without Him. God is the goal and focus. Heaven is simply a sphere or dimension or an expression from where the government of God's rule is established and manifested.

The Body of Christ, which is the Church, is established on the principle of His kingdom. Without the kingdom the Church has no purpose. Once we loose the focus of His kingdom we have lost everything.

"But seek ye first the kingdom of God, and His righteousness; and all these things shall be added unto you" - (Matthew 6:33).

More than anything else, we must put God's work first and do what He wants. His kingdom must become our priority.

Be concerned about His kingdom and what has His approval, then the other things will be yours as He has provided.

The apostolic and prophetic ministries are tools for His kingdom to be established in every sphere on earth as the Church is equipped and grows into the fullness of His image. Those who proclaim to be an apostolic or prophetic ministry must express the principles of God's kingdom, because there is no other message that the New Testament apostles and prophets preached, except the message of the kingdom of God.

The primary gospel of Jesus Christ is the message of the kingdom. If Jesus Christ is the pattern for the New Testament Church, then our message must be the same gospel of the kingdom.

When the Lord Jesus came to earth, His first proclamation was; *'repent for the kingdom of God is here'*. This was the only message He preached, and He declared that this is the purpose for which He was sent by the Father. This was also the message He commissioned His disciples (apostles) as He sent them out to preach.

"From then on, Jesus began to preach and to say, "Repent, because the kingdom from heaven is near!" - (Matthew 4:17 ISV).

"And He (Jesus) said unto them, **I must preach the kingdom of God** to other cities also: *for therefore am I sent*" - (Luke 4:43).

"And Jesus went about all Galilee, teaching in their synagogues, and **preaching the gospel of the kingdom,** and healing all manner of sickness and all manner of disease among the people" - (Matthew 4:23).

"And Jesus went about all the cities and villages, teaching in their synagogues, and **preaching the gospel of the kingdom**, and healing every sickness and every disease among the people" - (Matthew 9:35).

"Now after that John was put in prison, **Jesus came into Galilee, preaching the gospel of the kingdom of God**, And saying, The time is fulfilled, and the kingdom of God is at hand: repent ye, and believe the gospel" - (Mark 1:14-15).

"And it came to pass afterward, that He (Jesus) went throughout every city and village, preaching and shewing the glad tidings of the kingdom of God: and the twelve were with Him" - (Luke 8:1).

"Then He called His twelve disciples together, and gave them power and authority over all devils, and to cure diseases. ***And He sent them to preach the kingdom of God***, and to heal the sick" - (Luke 9:1).

"These twelve (apostles) Jesus sent forth, and commanded them, saying....**And as ye go, preach, saying, The kingdom of heaven is at hand**" - (Matthew 10:5, 7).

The central theme of the message of the kingdom of God is "JESUS". The kingdom is about the King. Jesus is the King. We must continue to emphasize Jesus in our message. If we miss the focus of Jesus in the message, then we have lost the essence of the message, and have not preached the gospel. The gospel must be *christocentric*. Christ should be the center and the only focus of the message. Whenever the message of the kingdom is preached it must activate the Christ in us and release us into the reality of our new creation in Him. Any gospel message and revelation that is preached which obscures this truth is inaccurate and false, because it obscures God's self revelation to us.

The proclamation of the gospel of self worth, fortune, personal achievements, destiny and so forth as the primary focus, at the expense of Christ is not the message. We cannot continue to preach only on material things and call it the gospel of the kingdom. We must be very careful not to prostitute the ministry and manipulate the people with deception because of fortune and riches.

The message of the kingdom of God is foundational to the building of God's house. Once we lay hold of the revelation of the kingdom and the concept of it, then we can begin to advance in other areas and fulfill our part in establishing and advancing God's will on earth as it is in heaven.

Earth's Redemption & Man:

"And God said, *Let us make man in our image, after our likeness: and let them have dominion* over the fish of the sea, and over the fowl of the air, and over the cattle, and over all the earth, and over every creeping thing that creepeth upon the earth" - (Genesis 1:26).

The first intent of God for man was for him to have dominion (rule) over all things on earth. This was the first principle God set in place that is fundamental in His order - The establishing of His kingdom (God's rule) on earth.

Man was created in the image of God to be like God, and for him (man) to rule and reign over all things on earth just as He (God) is in the heavens.

We are created to be the expression and representative of God's kingly rule and authority upon the earth.

To be created in God's image and likeness means that we are to have the same nature and characteristics of His righteousness, holiness, authority and sovereignty which is continually being renewed in full knowledge with the image of the one who created it.

"However, you were taught to have a new attitude (thinking, mindset). You were also taught to become a new person (God's Image) created to be like God, truly righteous and holy" - (Ephesians 4:23-24 GW).

"(We) have put on the new *man,* which is renewed in knowledge after the image of Him that created him" - (Colossians 3:10).

God is a Spirit with an endless life that is eternal. If man was created by God to be like Him here on earth, then man is an eternal spirit-being in God's class, with an endless spirit life that is destined to rule on earth. God's desire is that man should have dominion over the earth, and establish His governmental rule (kingdom) upon the earth as it is in heaven (Gen. 1:26-28, Matthew 6:9-10).

We must grasp this concept that, as God is in Heaven, so has He made us to be on earth. He is the El-lohim that rules in and from the heaven, but He has made us *gods* in the earth to rule the earth according to His will in heaven. We are created by God to be a part of this class of the El-lohim family; this is an awesome reality of who we were created to be.

For some reason, we have tried to change God into our depraved likeness, and we have reduced Him in our imaginations. This has created a false hope in the Church, and an expectation of what we think the plan of God is about.

Our imagination has become a hindrance to the purposes of God in the Church, and it has affected the advancement of the kingdom of God in and through us.

Our mindset is now a stronghold (2 Corinthians 10:3-6). We must allow the Holy Spirit to take its place in us, first in our mind, to change and transform the way we think (Ephesians 4:23).

It is absolute ignorance to think less of ourselves in Him, because the original status of who we were, and all we were created to be has been restored back to us in Christ Jesus through His finished work on the cross. This is the purpose and reality for our new creation.

"For whom He did foreknow, He also did predestinate to be conformed to the image of His Son, that He might be the firstborn among many brethren" - (Romans 8:29).

In being all God wants us to be, we must remember that God's greatest desire is for us to be conformed to the image of Christ. God doesn't just want us to come to Him; He wants us to be like Him.

Who we are has been hidden through the ages, but God is now unveiling our true identity to us by revelation. One of the greatest discoveries apart from knowing the Lord is to know who we are.

We cannot find purpose without discovering our value in Christ.

God created the earth for man, and it holds a place in the plan and purpose of God. Man was an integral part of God's plan for the whole of creation. The earth has no purpose without man, because it was created to be inhabited by man.

"For thus says the LORD, who created the heavens (He is God!), who formed the earth and made it (He established it; He did not create it empty *(He didn't create it for chaos),* He formed it to be inhabited!): "I am the LORD, and there is no other" - (Isaiah 45:18 ESV).

The purpose of God for the earth has not failed, neither has He given up on His intent. It is still the same today as it was in the beginning.

"And the devil said to Him (Jesus), "I will give You all this domain (kingdom) and its glory; ***for it has been handed over to me,*** and I give it to whomever I wish" - (Luke 4:6 NASB).

Man's authority and dominion was relinquished by Adam to the devil in the Garden of Eden in Genesis Chapter 3 through his ignorance and act of disobedience that led to his fall. It was handed over to the devil by Adam.

The good news (gospel) is that all (power, glory, authority, dominion, kingdoms) that was handed over to the devil by Adam has been restored back to us through Christ Jesus. The kingdom and all its power and glory has been restored back through Christ Jesus. What a joy to know who we are and what we are in Christ Jesus!

Everything we are, and that which was lost in Adam including our dominion heritage; in Christ Jesus, who is the *last* Adam ALL is restored to us.

Anything less is a lie from the devil, and it is not kingdom. I refuse a lesser life of oppression, suffering, pain, sickness, disease and a second-class citizenship; I choose an ever increasing life as a New Creation. I am a citzen of the kingdom of God, and I have all the benefits of God's kingdom as an entitlement.

The present condition and the desolation that is continually plaguing the earth with chaos and darkness is the result of man's corruption and the failure of the Church to rise to the occasion to understand the kingdom and to fulfill her purpose and destiny. For the earth to be restored the Church must first be restored, and for the Church to be restored, the revelation of God's purpose must first be restored to us. This is why there is a rediscovering, and the restoration of the message of the kingdom of God back to the Church, so the Church can function accurately in the pattern the Lord has ordered. This is the only hope for creation!

It took a man (Adam) to bring corruption upon the earth, so likewise it took a man (Christ) to bring redemption and restoration.

"As everyone dies because of Adam, so also everyone will be made alive because of Christ" - (1 Corinthians 15:22 GW).

A new man restored in the image of God is the instrument to bring transformation in the earth. The first chapter of the book of Genesis carries a whole lot of revelation that clearly define God's purpose for man and the earth:

1. *In the beginning* God created the universe (the heavens and earth) - (Genesis 1:1). *Everything* God created was good and perfect as we know.

2. The earth became a waste, void and desolate (Genesis 1:2a). If everything God created was good and perfect, then what happened between verse 1 and verse 2? How then did the earth become waste and void?

3. Darkness was upon the face of the deep (Genesis 1:2b). Darkness was the cause of earth's desolation. Darkness can be attributed to *ignorance,* the devil, evil or wickedness. Darkness is the absence of light and light means revelation (the Word of God - Psalm 119:105, 130). Where darkness exists there is no order (Job 10:22), so therefore order is a product of light.

"They have neither knowledge nor understanding, they walk about in darkness; all the foundations of the earth are shaken. I said, "You are gods, sons of the Most High, all of you" - (Psalm 82:5-6).

All the foundations of the earth are out of course (without order), because darkness (ignorance) prevails, which is the result of man not walking in the revelation (light) of God. If we want to see a change and order in the earth, the light (revelation) must first be restored.

4. And God said, 'Let light be;' and light is (Genesis 1:3). The first utterance (revealed Word) from God's mouth was 'let there be light', and the result was restoration and order being established as He spoke. Light means revelation which is the enlightenment of God's truth being revealed.

The key here is the need for revelation (light), because that is the only thing that can dispel darkness and bring change and order to the present condition of things.

5. Then God said, "Let us make man in our image, after our likeness. And let them have dominion...." - Genesis 1:26.

We can see here that light precedes man. The moment this was established, man was then set on the scene to walk in this light (revelation) so he can continue to keep the earth in divine order.

6. And God blessed them: and God said unto them, be fruitful, and multiply, and replenish the earth, and subdue it; and have dominion - Genesis 1:28.

The goal was for man to "**be fruitful, and multiply, and replenish the earth, and subdue it** (have dominion over the earth). <u>Man was created by God for this purpose</u>. This goal of God has not changed!

Genesis chapter 1 accounts for the revelation of man's beginning, but not the beginning of all things, because we can see that the earth itself existed before the genesis of man. Something happened to the earth to cause it to be desolated by darkness.

It is important to note the word **"replenish (re-plenish)"**. <u>The prefix **"re"** means to do it again</u>. Something happened to the earth and it was turned into a formless mass cloaked in darkness, and void. The earth was thus destroyed and reduced to this state by the evil one (satan and his demonic spirits of darkness) which were cast down from heaven to the earth (Isaiah 14:12-17), but <u>the goal of God in placing man on earth was to restore the earth</u>. Man's assignment was to **"re-plenish"** the earth as he dominates and rules over all things.

The establishment of the kingdom of God in the earth is a divine restoration committed to man to bring the earth back into order as it was in the beginning before it was destroyed and reduced into this formless mass of Genesis 1:2. The sovereignty of the kingdom of God has been from the beginning and the desire of God is for man to rule over all things.

The manifestation of God in the earth in the form of Jesus Christ (the God-Man), was for the purpose of restoring man back to his original state as it was in the beginning of the age before the fall. To make us a Spirit-Being, immortal, created and made in the likeness of God to have dominion over all things in the earth realm. This was Adam's original realm and purpose. This is why if any man be in Christ, he is a new creature restored to the image of God (2 Corinthians 5:17). A restoration takes place in our spirit that affects our being so we can now fulfill our original purpose on earth.

If we can comprehend the truth of God's goal for man's creation and his original purpose and place in the garden, then we will realize the purpose for our salvation, because the aim has never been for God to prepare man with an escapism mentality, but for him to bring heaven to earth (Matthew 6:10), to see His kingdom restored and established in the earth.

In examining Genesis chapter 1:26-28, you will realize God never blessed and commanded Adam to exercise dominion over the woman or other human beings, but for him to have stewardship and responsibility over the created order of things. With this understanding, <u>we need to be conscious of how we exercise our dominion mandate so we don't engage ourselves</u>

in trying to dominate and control other human beings and call it kingdom. We are made to influence the created order - all things, according to God's will.

"Then God blessed them and said, **"Be fruitful and multiply. Fill the earth and govern it.** Reign over the fish in the sea, the birds in the sky, and all the animals that scurry along the ground." - (Genesis 1:28 NLT).

When the gospel of the kingdom is not accurately proclaimed, then our authority is abandoned or abused.

"For the earnest expectation of the creature waiteth for the manifestation of the sons of God. For the creature was made subject to vanity, not willingly, but by reason of Him who hath subjected the same in hope, Because the creature itself also shall be delivered from the bondage of corruption into the glorious liberty of the children of God. For we know that the whole creation groaneth and travaileth in pain together until now" - (Romans 8:19-22).

Creation is earnestly looking out with eager longing for the revelation of God's new creation - the Sons of God. This new creation is to be revealed here on earth and they are the only hope for earth's deliverance. God's plan is that the Sons of God will be the instrument to set creation free from the servitude of corruption.

But how can we bring deliverance and freedom when we don't understand our identity and know who we are in Him as the Sons of God? How can we have dominion and rule when we don't know our purpose on earth?

Dominion begins from within. We must first be able to rule over our thought process to be able to overcome and rule without. We must be able to rule over ourselves to rule with Him. To govern takes an internal process of aligning our thoughts to His will.

"Do not be conformed to this world, but continually be transformed by the renewing of your minds so that you may be able to determine what God's will is—what is proper, pleasing, and perfect" - (Romans 12:2 ISV).

When the mind is elevated and renewed in the way of God, our influence in the environment will shift to bring a significant impact, because we cannot have the manifestation of the kingdom of God within us without the transformation of the environment.

It is like light and salt. It impacts and effects change whenever, and whatever it is applied to.

"Ye are the salt of the earth: but if the salt have lost his savour, wherewith shall it be salted? it is thenceforth good for nothing, but to be cast out, and to be trodden under foot of men. Ye are the light of the world. A city that is set on an hill cannot be hid. Neither do men light a candle, and put it under a bushel, but on a candlestick; and it giveth light unto all that are in the house. Let your light so shine before men, that they may see your good works, and glorify your Father which is in heaven" - (Matthew 5:13-16).

We are not born again only to enter the kingdom; but it is Father's delight to also give us the kingdom.

"Fear not, little flock; for it is your Father's good pleasure to give you the kingdom" - (Luke 12:32).

"Wherefore we receiving a kingdom which cannot be moved, let us have grace, whereby we may serve God acceptably with reverence and godly fear" - (Hebrews 12:28).

The grace of God is needed to enable us to receive the kingdom and it must be accepted with reverence and godly fear.

Suggested Reading:
Apostolic Strategies for Kingdom Reformation - Series 1
(The Message of the Kingdom & The Goal of God)
Author: Israel Onoriobe

The Family Order

"The Institution Of Divine Fatherhood & Sonship"

"For this cause I bow my knees unto the Father of our Lord Jesus Christ, Of whom the whole family in heaven and earth is named" - (Ephesians 3:14-15).

"The subject of "Spiritual Fathering" has become popular and many are making declarations concerning this subject without a clear revelation of the heart of the Lord. Here an excellent presentation delineating the process of God in restoring one of the most fundamental principles in this season of God. The choices are between the restoration of fathers and sons, and a curse resting upon the geography (Malachi 4:5-6). The fact that some take upon themselves the title of 'father' does not make it so, because only God calls or names fathers. Earth is not authorized to do this. There are things that the Lord reserves for Himself and not for another. Though it is acceptable to recognize and call someone in the natural your father, yet the same does not apply in the spiritual. Only God bring someone into that relationship and completes the processing necessary to allow someone to be declared by Heaven as a father in the earth realm".

Apostle John M. Boney
(Excerpt from the "Foreword" of my Book "The Process of Transition").

Chapter Six

The Family Order
(The Disclosing of Sonship)

The current season we are living in as the Church is characterized by three concepts, which form a pattern established by the Lord for His Church:

1. *The Foundation of the Apostolic & Prophetic - Ephesians 2:20-22.*
2. *Kingdom of God - (God's Priority) - Matthew 6:10, 33.*
3. *Fathering & Sonship - Malachi 4:5-6.*

The pattern God intends for His Church and His people is to be established as a strong influential apostolic and prophetic New Testament Church; walking with kingdom of God understanding and perspective - (pursuing God's priority - Matthew 6:10, 33); and being **established as a spiritual family in the order of Father and sons.**

We cannot deny the fact that the heaven and the earth is established on the divine order of family under the fatherhood of God, who is the Father of our Lord Jesus Christ, His firstborn Son among many children. This family in heaven and on earth functions on the concept and principle of Father and sons. This concept of Father and sons is an established pattern that can be seen throughout the scriptures as God relates with His people and with the Church as a family. It reveals the fact that God is a family oriented God. This makes family a priority in the heart of God, and in His plan and purposes for His people.

"For this cause I bow my knees unto the Father of our Lord Jesus Christ, of whom the whole family in heaven and earth is named" - (Ephesians 3:14-15).

"For whom He did foreknow, He also did predestinate to be conformed to the image of His Son, that He might be the first-born among many brethren" - (Romans 8:29).

If there is a family in heaven, it establishes the heavenly pattern, and it reflects the model the Church is designed to operate in.

From the beginning of the human race you will discover that a *family concept* was established as a fundamental principle among the Patriarch. They were not only fathers over sons; they were also called the sons of God with an Eternal Father.

Adam was the son of God (The Eternal Father).

"Which was the son of Enos, which was the son of Seth, which was the son of **Adam, which was the son of God**" - (Luke 3:38).

We are the sons of God.

"But as many as received Him, to them gave He power to become the sons of God, even to them that believe on His name" - (John 1:12).

"For as many as are led by the Spirit of God, they are the sons of God. For ye have not received the spirit of bondage again to fear; but ye have received the Spirit of adoption, whereby we cry, Abba, Father. The Spirit itself beareth witness with our spirit, that we are the children of God" - (Romans 8:14).

".....ye are sons, God hath sent forth the Spirit of His Son into your hearts, crying, Abba, Father" - (Galatians 4:6).

"Behold, what manner of love the Father hath bestowed upon us, that we should be called the sons of God: therefore the world knoweth us not, because it knew Him not. Beloved, now are we the sons of God, and it doth not yet appear what we shall be: but we know that, when He shall appear, we shall be like Him; for we shall see Him as He is" - (1 John 3:1-2).

The Church is a spiritual family that is established upon the covenant principle of spiritual fathering and sonship - Jeremiah 31:1-9.

"I write not these things to shame you, but as my beloved sons I warn you. For though ye have ten thousand instructors in Christ, yet have ye not many fathers: for in Christ Jesus I have begotten you through the gospel. Wherefore I beseech you, be ye followers of me" - (1 Corinthians 4:14-16).

"I (Jehovah) will be a Father unto you, and ye shall be my sons and daughters, saith the Lord Almighty" - (2 Corinthians 6:18 - emphasis is mine).

Peter was the spiritual father of Marcus, whom he regarded as a son.

"The church that is at Babylon, elected together with you, saluteth you; and so doth Marcus my son" - (1 Peter 5:13).

Paul was the spiritual father of Timothy, Titus and Onesimus, whom he regarded as sons and recommended them as faithful in the Lord and in the gospel.

"For this cause have I sent unto you Timotheus, who is my beloved son, and faithful in the Lord, who shall bring you into remembrance of my ways which be in Christ, as I teach every where in every church" - (1 Corinthians 4:17).

"But I trust in the Lord Jesus to send Timotheus shortly unto you, that I also may be of good comfort, when I know your state. For I have no man likeminded, who will naturally care for your state. For all seek their own, not the things which are Jesus Christ's. But ye know the proof of him, that, as a son with the father, he hath served with me in the gospel" - (Philippians 2:19-22).

"Unto Timothy, my own son in the faith: Grace, mercy, and peace, from God our Father and Jesus Christ our Lord" - (1 Timothy 1:2).

"To Titus, mine own son after the common faith: Grace, mercy, and peace, from God the Father and the Lord Jesus Christ our Saviour" - (Titus 1:4).

"I beseech thee for my son Onesimus, whom I have begotten in my bonds" - (Philemon 1:10).

As a matter of fact, those who could not show their pedigree were excluded from the heritage of the covenant and priesthood, and were considered polluted.

"And these were they which went up from Telmelah, Telharsa, Cherub, Addan, and Immer: but they could not shew their father's house, and their seed, whether they were of Israel: The children of Delaiah, the children of Tobiah, the children of Nekoda, six hundred fifty and two. And of the children of the priests: the children of Habaiah, the children of Koz, the children of Barzillai; which took a wife of the daughters of Barzil lai the Gileadite, and was called after their name: These sought their register among those that were reckoned by genealogy, **but they were not found: therefore were they, as polluted, put from the priesthood**. And the Tirshatha said unto them, that they should not eat of the most holy things, till there stood up a priest with Urim and with Thummim" - (Ezra 2:59-63).

What is missing in the 21st Century Church is the establishment of true apostolic and prophetic fathers and sons who are in alignment with the pattern of the heavenly family, and pursuing God's priority - His kingdom. We are missing this heavenly pattern and therefore missing the apostolic foundation and the Due Order of God for His Church as a family.

As stated in Chapter One, 'the place of true Apostolic Father's in today's Church and society cannot be overemphasized. This is a fatherless generation that is breaching the Spirit and releasing a curse. We have failed to see the important need for spiritual fathers and sonship principle, and the pattern the Lord has established for His Church as a family, because the devil wants us to be blind to this eternal truth, so he can hinder our maturity and full manifestation as the Sons of God that the world is waiting for'.

God is our Father. Nevertheless, He has pre-ordained certain men within the Body to express His Fatherhood in the earth, and to establish and strengthen the spiritual family of sons. Spiritual fathering is a transcending grace that flows from God through those He has called and sent specifically for this mandate, to raise and establish the sons of God in His purpose and pattern.

"My little children, of whom I travail in birth again until Christ be formed in you" – (Galatians 4:19).

Spiritual fathering does not shape us into the image of any man, but creates the mode for the formation of the image of Christ in us. This is the purpose of God as He has predestined us to be conformed to the image of His Son, Jesus Christ.

"God knew what He was doing from the very beginning. He decided from the outset to shape the lives of those who love Him along the same lines as the life of His Son. The Son stands first in the line of humanity He restored. We see the original and intended shape of our lives there in Him. After God made that decision of what His children should be like, He followed it up by calling people by name. After He called them by name, He set them on a solid basis with Himself. And then, after getting them established, He stayed with them to the end, gloriously completing what He had begun" – (Romans 8:29-30 MSG).

The principle of apostolic fathering and spiritual mentoring is a unique technology that carries an unusual grace and impartation that cannot be acquired anywhere. It is a dimension of God's grace that is released to us through spiritual fathering, because apostolic fathers "birth things" and also "establish things" in sons. It all depends on the level where we are in our spiritual journey in life and ministry.

"And he shall go before his face in the spirit and power of Elijah, to turn the hearts of the fathers to the children, and the disobedient to walk in the wisdom of the just; to make ready for the Lord a people prepared for Him" – (Luke 1:17 ASV).

The primary purpose for spiritual fathering is to make ready a people prepared for the Lord. We must not miss this central truth of spiritual fathering and reject the process of our transition, as the pathway into His fullness is revealed to us.

The Lord is seeking for a glorious Church – a people who have been conformed into the express image of His Son.

"A father of the fatherless, and a judge of the widows, is God in His holy habitation. **God setteth the solitary in families:** he bringeth out those which are bound with chains: but the rebellious dwell in a dry land" - (Psalm 68:5-6).

It is the Lord who determines your father and establishes you into the family He has ordained for you to fulfill His purpose. It is not your prerogative to choose your own spiritual father, or to call people your spiritual sons. This is only done by the sovereign act of God.

The Manifestation Of The Sons Of God:

"The Spirit Himself [thus] testifies together with our own spirit, [assuring us] that we are children of God. And if we are [His] children, then we are [His] heirs also: heirs of God and fellow heirs with Christ [sharing His inheritance with Him]; only we must share His suffering if we are to share His glory. [But what of that?] For I consider that the sufferings of this present time (this present life) are not worth being compared with **the glory that is about to be revealed to us and in us and for us and conferred on us!** For [even the whole] creation (all nature) waits expectantly and longs earnestly for God's sons to be made known [waits for the revealing, the disclosing of their sonship]. For the creation (nature) was subjected to frailty (to futility, condemned to frustration), not because of some intentional fault on its part, but by the will of Him Who so subjected it—[yet] with the hope.

That nature (creation) itself will be set free from its bondage to decay and corruption [and gain an entrance] into the glorious freedom of God's children. We know that the whole creation [of irrational creatures] has been moaning together in the pains of labor until now. And not only the creation, but we ourselves too, who have and enjoy the firstfruits of the [Holy] Spirit [a foretaste of the blissful things to come] groan inwardly as we wait for the redemption of our bodies [from sensuality and the grave, which will reveal] our adoption (our manifestation as God's sons)" - (Romans 8:16-23 Amplified Bible - AMP).

The joyful anticipation deepens, as pregnant creation anxiously waits for that moment of the glorious manifestation of the sons of God. All of creation (nature) will be delivered from corruption, and gain entrance into glorious liberty as the sons of God are fully manifested. This is God's will and purpose for us and the earth.

From time immemorial, there has been enmity and conflict between the seed of the woman and the devil. The prophetic declaration is that the "seed" of the woman, which is Christ, will bruise the head of the serpent, (and have dominion), and the "seed" of the serpent shall bruise his heel.

"And the LORD God said unto the serpent, Because thou hast done this, thou art cursed above all cattle, and above every beast of the field; upon thy belly shalt thou go, and dust shalt thou eat all the days of thy life: And <u>I will put enmity between thee and the woman, and between thy seed and her seed; it shall bruise thy head, and thou shalt bruise his heel</u>" - (Genesis 3:14-15).

This conflict has been visible through the ages, as the enemy has sought to kill the seed of the woman in order to stop the purpose of God and the redemption of God's people.

This was the case with Moses who was a proper child (seed) – (Hebrews 11:23), and Pharaoh the King, who was a type of a ruling demonic deity over Egypt, he tried to kill Moses from birth, but God preserved him to fulfill His purpose to bring out a people who became a nation to serve God - Exodus 1:15-22.

Another case was the queen mother, Athaliah, who was a counselor of wickedness, leading her son king Ahaziah and the people of Jerusalem to walk in the ways of the house of Ahab. **She arose and destroyed all the royal seed of the house of Judah,** because the house of Ahaziah had no power to keep the kingdom - (2 Chronicles 22:10-12), but Joash the son of Ahaziah was hidden in the house of God, so that Athaliah could not kill him. He was seven years old when he began to reign, as the LORD has said of the sons of David (2 Chronicles 23:3). God preserved Joash as a royal seed of the house of Judah from the destruction, because the death of Joash would have been the complete elimination of the seed of David, from whence Jesus Christ is. Joash did that which was right in the sight of the LORD all the days of Jehoiada the priest - (2 Chronicles 24:1-2).

"And when thy days be fulfilled, and thou shalt sleep with thy fathers, I will set up thy seed after thee, which shall proceed out of thy bowels, and I will establish his kingdom" - (2 Samuel 7:12).

Jesus the Son of God, who was made of the seed of David according to the flesh, was also known as Christ, the seed of Abraham (Romans 1:3-4, Galatians 3:16). Herod the king attempted to destroy the Seed (Jesus Christ) when he ordered the death of all the children under the age of two in Bethlehem, because he heard that a Governor, King of the Jews, and a ruler of the people of Israel was born - Matthew 2:1-23.

This spiritual conflict continues to rage until this day in order to stop the manifestation of the sons of God in the earth, but God is always faithful to the covenant of His word and His promise to bring it to fulfillment.

"For the kingdom is the LORD'S: and He is the governor among the nations.....A seed shall serve Him; it shall be accounted to the Lord for a generation. They shall come, and shall declare His righteousness unto a people that shall be born, that He hath done this" - (Psalm 22:28; 30-31).

This is one of the prophetic chapters of the book of Psalms written by David, as it related to Christ, and His seed, which is a generation that will proclaim His righteousness and His finished work.

This was a promise of a "seed" that is coming, which will be a posterity in the earth of a generation of people that will serve the Lord and declare His righteousness (His kingdom). The kingdom of God is righteousness (Romans 14:17).

God is seeking for a generation (a seed) that will finish His purpose and accomplish His will on the earth. This Seed is not an ordinary generation. *This Seed is an eternal generation* that is born of the Spirit of Christ. They are the sons of God who will be manifested. They are the Christ's of God on earth, and the will of the Lord will succeed through them.

"He was taken from prison and from judgment: and ***who shall declare his generation***? for he was cut off out of the land of the living: for the transgression of my people was he stricken. And he made his grave with the wicked, and with the rich in his death; because he had done no violence, neither was any deceit in his mouth. Yet it pleased the LORD to bruise him; he hath put him to grief: when thou shalt make his soul an offering for sin, ***he shall see his seed***, he shall prolong his days, and ***the pleasure of the LORD shall prosper in his hand***" - (Isaiah 53:8-10).

The Missing Generation – "The 42nd Generation After Jesus":

One of God's goals is that He is seeking for a generation that will finish His purpose and plan in the earth, this I believe is the "Missing Generation" that is being revealed.

"So all the generations from Abraham to David are fourteen generations; and from David until the carrying away into Babylon are fourteen generations; and from the carrying away into Babylon unto Christ are fourteen generations" - (Matthew 1:17).

The study of Matthew Chapter One about the generation of Jesus Christ, the seed of David, the seed of Abraham, is significant in revealing a generation that is called **"Christ"**. Verse 17 speaks of a total of 42 generations **(14 + 14 + 14 = 42)**. The last generation, which is number 42 on the list, is called **"Christ"**.

Here, the 42nd generation that is called "Christ" is not referring to Jesus Christ as some may think, because if you do the counting down from verse 2, you will realize that Jesus Christ is Number 41 on the list of generation from Abraham, but there is another generation after Jesus Christ that is 42nd on the list that Matthew 1:17 called "Christ".

Who is this "Christ", the 42nd Generation after Jesus?

First of all, the word **"Christ"** comes from ***"Christos",*** a Greek word meaning "the Anointed One" or "the Chosen One", that is, "the Messiah", an epithet of Jesus in the New Testament - Acts 2:36.

To the surprise of some, **"Christ"** is not Jesus' last name (surname). **"Christ" is also referred to as a corporate entity - a many-membered body, which is the Church**. *It is from this understanding that the early Church was called "the Body of Christ".*

"For as the body is one, and hath many members, and all the members of that one body, being many, are one body: **so also is Christ**" - (1 Corinthians 12:12).

"For the body is not one member, but many" - (1 Corinthians 12:14).

"Now ye are the body of Christ, and members in particular" - (1 Corinthians 12:27).

"And He (Jesus) is the head of the body, the Church...." - (Colossians 1:18).

Let us make the connection here from the above scriptures:

Christ is the Head, which is Jesus.
Christ is the Body, the Church.

The "head" and the "body" are ONE. They are the same and identical. Christ is a Corporate Man.

We are the Body - We are the Church, which is the Christ.

We are a chosen generation (1 Peter 2:9). We are the "Christ", the Missing Generation, and the 42nd generation after Jesus.

The desire of God is that we as the Church would grow into the fullness of the stature of Christ; to come into this ONENESS of a perfect man in Him as the sons of God.

"And He gave some, apostles; and some, prophets; and some, evangelists; and some, pastors and teachers; For the perfecting of the saints, for the work of the ministry, for the edifying of the body of Christ: Till we all come in the unity of the faith, and of the knowledge of the Son of God, unto **a perfect man, unto the measure of the stature of the fulness of Christ**" - (Ephesians 4:11-13).

God's ultimate purpose is for us (the Church) to be One with Christ, and to have the same form as the image of His Son Jesus. We were created to have the same image and likeness (Genesis 1:26).

This is who we were before the fall of humanity through the first man, Adam, whose sin of disobedience has changed our nature and corrupted our original identity, but Jesus Christ the last Adam has restored to us everything we lost in the first Adam, and this includes our identity as Christ's.

This is why the five fold ministry of the apostles, the prophets, the evangelists, the pastors and the teachers must be delivered from the religiosity of the traditions of men, and be released in the Church to function in its true purpose and destiny to prepare and equip the Church to become the desire and intent God has purposed for us.

The Church of Jesus Christ is the generation of Christ (the sons of God) that is to be manifested in the earth, who will come forth in the fullness of the true image of God.

The earnest expectation of creation is waiting for the **Christ – "the manifested sons of God"** to be revealed, who will deliver creation from bondage - Romans 8:19-21.

"This is true because He already knew His people and had already ***appointed them to have the same form as the image of His Son***. Therefore, His Son is the firstborn among many children. He also called those whom He had already appointed. He approved of those whom He had called, and He gave glory to those whom He had approved of" - (Romans 8:29-30).

There is a greater depth of revelation and insight in this that we must grasp to discover who we really are as Christ, the sons of God, and seek to walk in this glory and destiny of God's purpose that He has preordained for us before the foundation of the world. God's desire is that we have ***the same form as the image of His Son***. As Christ is, so He desires that we be.

This missing generation, the Christ that is being unfolded to creation is a corporate company of people begotten of the Lord Jesus Christ Himself, who are shaped into His image.

They are the sons of God that will bear His glory upon the earth.
They are the Overcomer - They have overcome the wicked one.
They are breakthrough saints with a finishing mindset to accomplish God's will.
They are consumed with the vision of Zion, to become the dwelling place of God.
They know the ways of God through divine relationship with Christ.
They are dead to sin, self and the desires of this world.
They are people who are NOT subject to the institutional church.
They are the true reflection of the Body of Christ, called out of the system of Babylon.

Suggested Reading:
The Process of Transition
(Understanding The Pathways of God)
Author: Israel Onoriobe

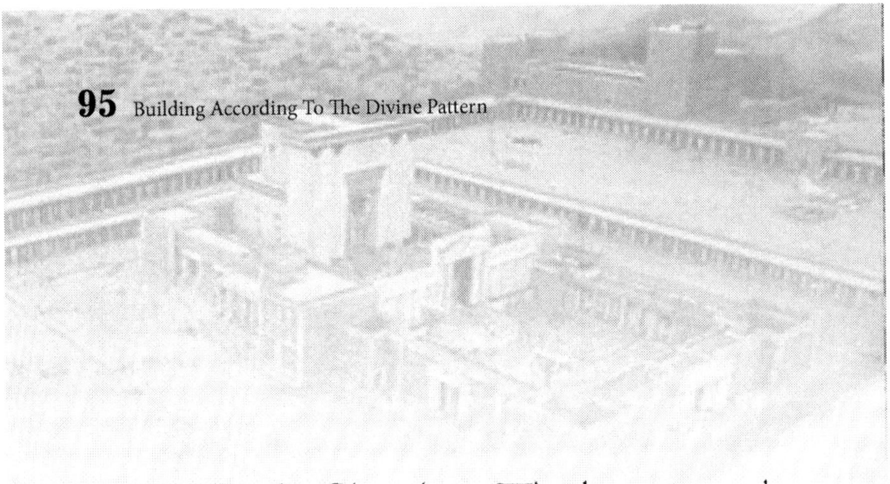

The Body Church vs. The Institutional Church

"A Focus Of Rediscovering The Apostolic Pattern Of The New Testament Church"

"I will build my Church; and the gates of hell shall not prevail against it" - Jesus Christ.

"Now ye are the body of Christ, and members in particular" (1 Corinthians 12:27).

Chapter Seven

The Body Church vs The Institutional Church

"When Jesus came into the coasts of Caesarea Philippi, He asked his disciples, saying, Whom do men say that I the Son of man am? And they said, Some say that thou art John the Baptist: some, Elias; and others, Jeremias, or one of the prophets. He saith unto them, But whom say ye that I am? And Simon Peter answered and said, Thou art the Christ, the Son of the living God. And Jesus answered and said unto him, Blessed art thou, Simon Barjona: for flesh and blood hath not revealed it unto thee, but my Father which is in heaven. And I say also unto thee, That thou art Peter, and upon this rock I will build my church; and the gates of hell shall not prevail against it. And I will give unto thee the keys of the kingdom of heaven: and whatsoever thou shalt bind on earth shall be bound in heaven: and whatsoever thou shalt loose on earth shall be loosed in heaven" - (Matthew 16:13-19).

The danger we face in this present season is lack of insight and understanding of what the Church actually is, and the blueprint to accurately build the house of God according to His pattern. This has resulted in many building institutional organizations and denominations that are centered on the doctrinal understanding and traditions of men, rather than being established as an organism of divine life and revelational truth in Christ.

The Church being a physical structure and a religious organization as supposed by many; reflects ignorance of the purpose and the true meaning of the Church. The Greek word for "Church" is "Ecclesia". This means, "the called out ones", an assembly, a congregation or a group of people called out from the kingdom of darkness into the kingdom of God.

The Church of Jesus Christ is not a religious organization. It is an organism. It is a community of faith in Christ and the people of a kingdom. The Church is the people of the kingdom of God who are under God's dominion, and submitting to His will. The Church has never been a denomination or a physical building raised up somewhere in the city, but it is a realm of God's kingdom community that is embodied within a people, who have been called out of the world and out of a religious system. Therefore, the Church must function as a body of organism and not as an institutional organization that is set up by men.

The kingdom has never been about the building of an institution, but rather the building of a corporate people who are one in Christ. This corporate people are the Body of Christ, which is the embodiment and fullness of Jesus Christ.

"For as the body is one, and hath many members, and all the members of that one body, being many, are one body: so also is Christ. For by one Spirit are we all baptized into one body, whether we be Jews or Gentiles, whether we be bond or free; and have been all made to drink into one Spirit. For the body is not one member, but many....Now ye are the body of Christ, and members in particular" - (1 Corinthians 12:12-14, 27).

The Lord Jesus founded no institutional or religious organization, but He came as the Messiah, to call out a remnant of people who are held captive by a religious system, and to bring them into a relationship with His Father. He came to deliver people from the powers of darkness into His kingdom. He came to es tablish the kingdom of God.

There is a proliferation of denominations, organizational institutions, ministries, and magnificent buildings to which the name 'Church' is applied. The Church has been made to become an organized religion, rather than a relationship and an organic life with God. The scripture doesn't speak of such institutions and structures as the true Church of our Lord Jesus Christ. ***The Church has always been the people of God - The Body of Christ, not an organizational institution.*** The Church may have some organizational expression for administrative purposes, but the Church is first of all, a body of organism with a spiritual relationship with Christ and God the Father.

The declaration of the Lord Jesus to Peter was, *'upon this rock I will build my Church'*. Peter is not the Rock on which Jesus said the Church will be built, because the Church is not built on men. The Church is built on Jesus Christ. The Rock is the revelation of the TRUTH, which is Jesus Christ Himself. The Revelation of Jesus, the Son of the living God, is the foundational Rock on which the Church is established. There is no other foundation. (John 14:6, 1 Corinthians 10:4, Isaiah 28:16, 1 Corinthians 3:10-11, Ephesians 2:20-22).

When we understand the concept that God is building a "Body Church", and He alone will build His Church, then we can begin to realize that men cannot build His Church in their own ways. For the scripture clearly states, ***I (Jesus) will build my Church (Matthew 16:18)***. Anything that has been built by men is only an institutional church, except it is built according to the pattern of God. Only the Church that is built by Christ will stand against the prevailing force of the gates of hell.

The difference is clear!

Man builds institutions – God is growing a Body Church.

The tower of Babel is a reflection of an institution of what man builds, but the Church is a corporate Body of people that God is growing as a living organism (1 Corinthians 12:27).

Institutions are temporal – The Body Church is eternal, and will live forever.

In the consummation of all things, institutions will be destroyed just like the tower of Babel, because there will be a shaking (Hebrews 12:26-28) that will cause man-made systems and structures to be removed, but the Church that is established in the principles and pattern of the kingdom will remain - the gates of hell shall not prevail against it (Matthew 16:18, 2 Corinthians 4:18).

Institutions divide and alienate – The Body Church unites.

Denominations have brought segregation and banished people who do not conform to their system and doctrines, but the Body Church is a family unit based on relationship, with the headship of Jesus. The Body is one, and united in Him - Christ.

Institutions are mostly centered on doctrines – The Body Church is family oriented.

Denominational institutions are mostly centered on the doctrines of men which become the traditions of their belief system (Matthew 16:11-12), but the Body Church is a spiritual family that has a kingdom community mindset. The pattern of God is a family that is relational - Father and Sons. God is a family God.

"For this cause I bow my knees unto the Father of our Lord Jesus Christ, of whom the whole family in the heavens and on earth is named" - (Ephesians 3:14-15).

To the institutional church the principles and doctrines of the kingdom are a strange doctrine, because they have estranged themselves from Christ and His kingdom.

We are in a season of spiritual awakening, where the religious system will be in direct collision with the Body Church, because of the revelation of the kingdom of God. It will be like the manifestation of the Messiah (Jesus Christ) 2000 years ago. It was a shock to the religious system of His day as it was a direct confrontation to the religious sects and traditions of men - Mark 7:1-13.

Institutions are manipulated by men – The Body Church is administered by God.

Institutions are controlled by men who focus on positions and quest for titles to control the people and influence the system in instituting governments and laws that replicate democracy. They seek to be masters rather than servants. However, the Body Church functions apostolically with Jesus as the head - It is a theocratic government. The Body Church is not title oriented, but functions as a Body with members mutually serving one another. The effective functioning of the Body of Christ - the Church, is largely determined by the extent to which there exists a 'holding fast' to the head, which is Christ. For all that is in the 'head' to be transmitted to the whole body, there need to be a proper connection of the body to the head, which also implies submission. For increase to be transmitted from the head to the body, there must be a subjection of the body to the dictates of the head. If there is no submission, there can be no transmission of life and increase of God's grace.

The Institutional church is Democratic - The Body Church is Theocratic.

Democracy can be defined as a political system of government by which the people have an equal share of formal power. This principle of social equality is embodied in the concept of 'rule by the people', exercised either directly or through elected representatives. This concept empowers the majority to become the primary source of power. This is a form of government in which supreme power is vested in the people and exercised by the people.

Democracy has an autonomous mentality of self-governing. This is a means for the people to choose their leaders through a voting system. The effect of this is the absolute rejection of God's rule of law. The implementation of democracy within the Church is the carnal intent of man to achieve his rights by rebelling against the righteous government of God. For the most part, the system of government found in the institutional churches and some independent churches is an impediment to God's system of kingdom government which is theocratic. The pastoral leadership model and the board of directors established within and over the local church with the supreme power to elect and reject leadership is a hindrance to the New Testament type of apostolic presbytery. The government of God's kingdom is theocratic in nature! God does not need the vote of men to determine His rule and leadership.

The Body Church functions with an apostolic presbytery which is the New Testament pattern of leadership over the local assembly.

Institutions glorify men – The Body Church glorifies God.

Institutions are built as monuments of men's achievement to make a name for themselves like the tower of Babel and Absalom's monument (Genesis 11:4-5, 2 Samuel 18:18), but the Body Church glorifies God as a witness to His grace, because without Him we are nothing - *For in Him we live, and move, and have our being* (Acts 17:28a). "The institution church is man-centered, but the Body Church is God-centered".

The Institutional church is a 'One Man' ministry - The Body Church is A Team Ministry.

The institutional church is a 'One Man' ministry where he acts as the CEO and superstar, and he becomes the focus of all activities. Everything revolves around the man, but the Body Church is a team ministry which is a true reflection of an apostolic Church that is built according to God's pattern. The Body Church is organic and relational. Each part draws its strength from another's grace and it gives no room for the conflict of interest or competitiveness. The Church is a Body, and a body cannot function alone. It takes each part fitly joined together and working as one - 1 Corinthians 12:21-27.

The Institutional church is membership oriented - The Body Church is discipleship oriented.

The institutional church is a membership oriented organization because its vision functions with a pastoral model. It is engulfed in the ambition to gather members to build monuments and cathedrals without giving much priority to discipleship. The organized system of the institutional church is a problem, trying to raise members and supporters to influence their pursuit for positions, instead of discipling citizens for the kingdom.

The Body Church is a strong Antioch apostolic-type Church with a focus on building, raising, equipping and releasing kingdom disciples to do the work of the ministry. The strength and growth of the Church is tied to our capacity to make disciples and not members.

The question here is, are you laying stones (raising disciples - 1 Peter 2:5) to build a spiritual house for God, or are you gathering bricks (members together) to build a monument to make a name for yourself?

Institutional churches are focused on men's gifts - The Body Church is focused on the saints - equipping and maturing them.

The institutional church is built around men, and places dependence on the charisma (gifts) of the leaders, but the Body Church equips and empowers the saints to minister to the Body, and not the Body constantly dependent on the charisma of the leaders alone. When the saints can minister to each other and building one another up in Christ; it is a sign of true spiritual growth and maturity.

The institutional church desires "the things of God" - The Body Church desires "the will of God".

The institutional church is more concerned about *what they can get from God* - they always come with an open hand to receive. The focus and motivation is on meeting the needs of men; but the Body Church is more concerned with *what they can give to God* - they always come with an open heart to give (to do His will). The focus is on meeting the needs of God.

The Church is failing to fully embrace the supremacy of God's will and purpose. Instead, we are becoming self-centered. We place our welfare above the plans and the purpose of God. Without a kingdom mentality, we will desire the "things of God" more than the "will of God". The institutional church is need conscious, rather than God conscious. We have replaced His higher purpose with our personal goal of attaining His blessings and benefits, rather than seeking first His kingdom and His righteousness.

Genesis 1:28 says, "God blessed them - Adam and Eve". Why did He bless them? God blessed them to be fruitful and to multiply in order to fulfill His purpose to replenish the earth. *God does not just bless and anoint people - He blesses and anoints purpose*. God has no reason or purpose to bless and anoint a man if he is not going to profit and fulfill His primary purpose.

We must always put the plan and purpose of God first in our lives. Our relationships, our businesses and the ministry are not for our own personal benefit. We must see God's will beyond self.

"But seek ye first the kingdom of God, and His righteousness; and all these things shall be added unto you" - (Matthew 6:33).

Where is your priority? We must define and decide where our priority will be! Is it on the institutions that men are building, or on what God is presently doing in the earth through His Body Church that is built according to His pattern to advance His eternal kingdom?

The institutional mindset is a hindrance to the principles of the kingdom and the order of God, because it represents an old wineskin which is superfluous. The institutional church and all its religious structures and traditions cannot represent the pattern of God and His kingdom, except there is a paradigm shift and restructuring. The divine verdict is that "new wine must be put into fresh wineskin".

"And no man putteth new wine into old bottles; else the new wine will burst the bottles, and be spilled, and the bottles shall perish. But new wine must be put into new bottles; and both are preserved" - (Luke 5:37-38).

Jesus clearly distinguishes between the "new wine" and the "old wineskin". The new wine is something that is essential. The Church of today is refusing the essential and the new, which is the pattern of the kingdom, and holding unto the old wineskin that includes man-made traditions, old structures and patterns of doing things that are not accurate in this new season. We are failing to recognize that we have come into a new age and season in the kingdom of God that requires that we do away with the old wine and the old wineskin. God is a God of newness and renewal. We must transition our mind to embrace the fact that new things are being declared, and we need to receive the new things that God is pouring out upon us through the revelation of His kingdom. It is the reality of the Holy Spirit revealing new things and accurate patterns to us, and showing us things that are yet to come as promised in John 16:13.

"Behold, the former things are come to pass, and new things do I declare: before they spring forth I tell you of them. Sing unto the LORD a new song, and His praise from the end of the earth..." - (Isaiah 42:9-10a).

"Remember ye not the former things, neither consider the things of old. Behold, I will do a new thing; now it shall spring forth; shall ye not know it..." - (Isaiah 43:18–19a).

Changing the name of the ministry and adding Kingdom, Apostolic, Prophetic or subscribing to an apostolic network and ministry list does not address the old wineskin. It is like trying to patch an old garment with a piece of new garment, or it is like pouring new wine into an old wineskin.

"No man putteth a piece of new cloth unto an old garment, for that which is put in to fill it up taketh from the garment, and the rent is made worse. Neither do men put new wine into old bottles: else the bottles break, and the wine runneth out, and the bottles perish: but they put new wine into new bottles, and both are preserved" – (Matthew 9:16-17).

The old wineskin is also referring to humans; therefore change is required in our mindset, our motives and our character. The more excellent way of God is by submission and relationship with a true kingdom apostolic and prophetic ministry that is called out by Christ and allowing this ministry to completely uproot and destroy the old and to build and plant the DNA of the Father. That DNA becomes a new seed of the life of Christ in us. This may require a complete change of our ministry goal, structures, priority and sometimes the popular message and ministers we are accustomed to, and to embrace a fresh revelation and an accurate understanding of the gospel of the kingdom and the pattern of God.

Spiritual Birth Defect:

"There was a man of the Pharisees, named Nicodemus, a ruler of the Jews: The same came to Jesus by night, and said unto Him, Rabbi, we know that thou art a teacher come from God: for no man can do these miracles that thou doest, except God be with him. Jesus answered and said unto him, Verily, verily, I say unto thee, Except a man be born again, he cannot see the kingdom of God. Nicodemus saith unto Him, How can a man be born when he is old? can he enter the second time into his mother's womb, and be born? Jesus answered, Verily, verily, I say unto thee, Except a man be born of water and of the Spirit, he cannot enter into the kingdom of God. That which is born of the flesh is flesh; and that which is born of the Spirit is spirit. Marvel not that I said unto thee, Ye must be born again. The wind bloweth where it listeth, and thou hearest the sound thereof, but canst not tell whence it cometh, and whither it goeth: so is every one that is born of the Spirit. Nicodemus answered and said unto Him, How can these things be? Jesus answered and said unto him, Art thou a master of Israel, and knowest not these things? Verily, verily, I say unto thee, We speak that we do know, and testify that we have seen; and ye receive not our witness. If I have told you earthly things, and ye believe not, how shall ye believe, if I tell you of heavenly things? And no man hath ascended up to heaven, but He that came down from heaven, even the Son of man which is in heaven" - (John 3:1-13).

The problem with the present Church is the seed through which we have been birthed. The nature of the plant is greatly determined by the seed, and the outcome determined by the soil. We are the planting of God in His house; therefore the seed through which we are spiritually birthed must be the "incorruptible seed" and not corruptible seed. The incorruptible seed is the Word of God, which lives and abides forever. This incorruptible seed is the eternal truth of God that produces His life within us.

"Forasmuch as ye know that ye were not redeemed with corruptible things, as silver and gold, from your vain conversation received by tradition from your fathers; But with the precious blood of Christ, as of a lamb without blemish and without spot: Who verily was foreordained before the foundation of the world, but was manifest in these last times for you, Who by Him do believe in God, that raised Him up from the dead, and gave Him glory; that your faith and hope might be in God. Seeing ye have purified your souls in obeying the truth through the Spirit unto unfeigned love of the brethren, see that ye love one another with a pure heart fervently: Being born again, not of corruptible seed, but of incorruptible, by the word of God, which liveth and abideth for ever" - (1 Peter 1:18-13).

The majority of the people who profess to be believers have been spiritually birthed through the corruptible seed of religion and traditions from our forefathers. This has affected our concept of the intent and purposes of God for our salvation and for the kingdom of God.

We must allow God to kill that corruptible seed and the fruits it has produced in our lives and in the Church, so we can be rebirthed through the incorruptible seed to produce the life and fruits God has originally intended. This is a whole new process of repentance and becoming born again into His kingdom.

This might be frightening and disappointing to many who have come so far in their spiritual walk over the years, only to discover that they have been walking on the path of religion.

The question here is, do we endeavor to bend our thoughts to the scripture, or do we use the scripture to support our thoughts?

Rather than changing previous understanding of doctrines to align with the truth of God's Word, many have endangered themselves by clinging to the conclusions of their most respected teachers who they previously learned from. We must be willing to re-examine our doctrinal convictions and never bend scripture to fit our concepts.

I recalled an event with an Indian Brother who was in covenant relationship with me in South Africa. The first time I met him along with other leaders for a breakfast meeting, they were excited sharing with me a certain spiritual truth with which I did not agree. My Brother then said it was because I was not born again or filled with the Holy Spirit that is why I did not understand this truth and was not able to receive it. I was disappointed by his statement telling me that I wasn't born again or filled with the Holy Spirit, and I felt angry within me that he spoke to me in that manner, because I was convinced of my knowledge and understanding of the doctrine. Considering all my works and accomplishments for the Lord over the years as a minister of the gospel, and for him to tell me that I wasn't filled with the Holy Spirit. I left them in order not to continue in the debate and not to unleash my unrighteous anger. But interestingly, a few months later after a series of in-depth teachings and spiritual impartations of grace and revelation from my mentor and spiritual father whom I was accountable to, I received the exact same word. I now understood what my fellow ministers were saying, which in the beginning was contrary to what I had believed because of my up-bring in the doctrines and traditions of men that I was trapped in. That Indian Brother became a good covenant friend of mine, and we had the privilege of laboring together in South Africa and Australia before he went on to be with the Lord.

This was the same process with Nicodemus, who was born into Judaism and trapped in the religious traditions of his time, and could not know or understand the things the Lord was saying about 'seeing' and 'entering' into the Kingdom of God. He had a spiritual birth defect from his humanistic lineage of religion that affected his mindset and understanding - Isaiah 44:18, Romans 8:5-9.

Jesus then declared to him, ***"you must be born again of water and of the Spirit"***. Judaism and religious traditions could not understand what God was saying and doing, even though Nicodemus was a teacher and a prince among the rulers of his days.

Change is required in us and in the Church because of the necessity to build according to the pattern. Being established on the foundation of the apostles and prophets, and receiving the principles and pattern of the kingdom will always demand and produce change. The institutional church, outmoded traditions, old habits and inaccurate structures of churches and governments must be changed. Our priority must be set right. The religious church with the old structure and pattern of institutional government cannot bring forth the kingdom government of God. It is only the Church that is built according to the pattern of God that will manifest the kingdom of God, and become a dwelling place for God on earth.

God is going to shake the church system as He shakes the heavens and the earth (it is on-going) - Hebrews 12:26-29; and God will shut down so many strange and idolatrous places which are called churches and ministries, because His name and His glory is no longer there. God is pulling the plug. The show is over! Enough of this foolishness and ignorance, says the Lord!

A company of people is rising in the earth, and they are coming. O Earth, *Rejoice For Your Time Is Now!* Your redemption is at hand. Babylon is fallen, Babylon is fallen – The ungodly governmental system of the church is coming down and a new order is being raised. Rejoice in this that the Lord does. Selah!

The Pattern Of An Apostolic Community

"The Community Life Of An Apostolic & Prophetic Church"

"I know thy works, and thy labour, and thy patience, and how thou canst not bear them which are evil: and thou hast tried them which say they are apostles, and are not, and hast found them liars: And hast borne, and hast patience, and for my name's sake hast laboured, and hast not fainted. Nevertheless I have somewhat against thee, because thou hast left thy first love. Remember therefore from whence thou art fallen, and repent, and do the first works; or else I will come unto thee quickly, and will remove thy candlestick out of his place, except thou repent. But this thou hast, that thou hatest the deeds of the Nicolaitans, which I also hate. He that hath an ear, let him hear what the Spirit saith unto the churches; To him that overcometh will I give to eat of the tree of life, which is in the midst of the paradise of God" - (Revelation 2:2-7).

Chapter Eight

The Pattern Of An Apostolic Community

Let us begin with an overview of what a community is so we can look into the pattern of the New Testament Church; a pattern essential in building a strong kingdom Church that will have a significant influence and impact in society.

We can think of a community as a society of people with four elements:

(1) A culture of people living in proximity to each other, under the same conditions of life, sharing a common goal and knitted together.
(2) A people with common interests.
(3) A sharing by all alike and all having a common possession.
(4) A possession of a common character and nature.

Within these four elements that define a community, you will notice that the word ***'common'*** is general.

I want to briefly talk about each of these four elements of a community, so we can better understand and embrace the Church as an apostolic community of kingdom people, and as well see the pattern that the New Testament saints had as a community that made them significant in their day.

(1) A community is a culture of people living together, under the same conditions of life, sharing a common goal and knitted together.

This speaks of a family with a strong principle that cannot be divided by gender, race or any form of weakness. In a family, one loses independence, because a family is inter-dependent.

Also, your weakness may be my strength, and your strength may be my weakness, so we bear one another for the purpose of achieving a singular vision.

The Body of Christ - the Church, is the spiritual family of God on earth that should express a true community spirit of a kingdom people living as a family. To an extent we have failed to manifest this character of a family that is fundamental in the principle of a community like that reflected among the saints in the early Church.

(2) A community is a people with a common interest.

It is important to state here that as an apostolic community of kingdom people, our primary interest is to be a building block in the house of God for the advancement of His kingdom. This interest of the family to advance the kingdom of God must become our sole priority. We must have a common interest as citizens of the kingdom of God. The desire of the King must be our only interest, because in a kingdom the king's desire is the people's interest and priority.

The people in the land of Shinar in Genesis 11:1–9, revealed the principle and power of a community of people. They had a common interest in building a city and a tower that would stand as a great monument to their own self-glory, even though this desire was contrary to the desire of God. The reason they could do this was because of their common interest and goal, which brought them together as a community with one voice and purpose. This expression of a common interest and community spirit within them resulted in a great accomplishment on earth that only God could bring to an end because it did not reflect His will and pattern.

"And the LORD said, Behold, the people is one, and they have all one language; and this they begin to do: and now nothing will be restrained from them, which they have imagined to do." - (Genesis 11:6).

The dynamic of a community of kingdom people is that they can cause a release of supernatural power that will bring the imagination of their heart into manifestation according to God's will in order to see the kingdom of God established on earth. A community operating in the will of God will cause God's power to be manifested (Acts 4:32-35). When we walk with a community spirit and mindset, we have so much power at our disposal. This is why the enemy will fight to divide us so he can hinder the release of God's power through us. There is power in unity.

(3) A Community has a sharing by all alike, and all have a common possession.

This speaks of a family that is established on the principle of building with a genuine spirit of community, and having the same purpose based on mutual respect and care. This could be considered as a common-wealth.

The misappropriation of the gospel of prosperity and fortune has affected the mindset of God's people to overlook the responsibility of meeting the needs of those in the spiritual family to bring some level of equality. This has caused many within the Church to become a selfish group of people who place their faith on material things and who trust in the systems of men above the will of God and above their love for one another.

"And all that believed were together, and had all things common; And sold their possessions and goods, and parted them to all men, as every man had need." - (Acts 2:44-45).

(4) A Possession of a common character and nature.

If we claim to be a part of the community of God's kingdom as an apostolic people, then we should express the divine nature and character of God, because this is part of the inheritance we have received in the Lord. ***God is love, and love is God***. This is His character and nature. We cannot live like the wicked world with an unforgiving and passionless soul, and say we are Christ's.

"Dear friends, we must love each other because love comes from God. Everyone who loves has been born from God and knows God. The person who doesn't love doesn't know God, because God is love. God has shown us His love by sending His only Son into the world so that we could have life through Him. This is love: not that we have loved God, but that He loved us and sent His Son to be the payment for our sins. Dear friends, if this is the way God loved us, we must also love each other" - (1 John 4:7-11 GW).

"A new commandment I give unto you, That ye love one another; as I have loved you, that ye also love one another. By this shall all men know that ye are my disciples, if ye have love one to another" - (John 13:34-35).

God is holy. Holiness is the sum character of God. Our lifestyle and our conversation must be that of holiness and righteousness unto the Lord.

"Wherefore gird up the loins of your mind, be sober, and hope to the end for the grace that is to be brought unto you at the revelation of Jesus Christ; As obedient children, not fashioning yourselves according to the former lusts in your ignorance: But as He which hath called you is holy, so be ye holy in all manner of conversation; Because it is written, Be ye holy; for I am holy" - (1 Peter 1:13-16).

"What? know ye not that your body is the temple of the Holy Ghost which is in you, which ye have of God, and ye are not your own? For ye are bought with a price: therefore glorify God in your body, and in your spirit, which are God's" - (1 Corinthians 6:19-20).

The key to the four elements of community we have briefly touched is that it can only function by relationship - *with God and with one another*. An apostolic community is bound together in authentic relational fellowship. The core of an apostolic community is relationship which leads to fruitfulness. When these begin to exist among us, evangelism becomes effortless within the apostolic community. The point is that when we establish right relationships within the Body, Church growth and evangelism become common (Acts 2:47).

Many within the religious circle of the church do not understand relationship. The kingdom does not function without proper relationship that is expressed in covenant and commitment. God does not walk with any man except He brings him to a place of an established covenant relationship.

Investing quality time in our communication and relationship building is essential to develop covenant that will bring a true community mentality among the Body. We must give priority to this.

The breakdown of communication among the people resulted in them abandoning the project of building the city and tower of Babel. God had to break the covenant of community among them by confounding their language, so they could not understand one another's speech (Genesis 11:7-8).

As Keith Intrater put it in his book, **Covenant Relationship,**"*one of the most demanding duties a person can be engaged in is to communicate. Communication takes tremendous effort. The process of covenant takes communication and more communication*".

The Body Church is relational. The kingdom of God is relational. Therefore, we must be a relational people.

Let us consider some of the traits found in the New Testament Church that gives an expression of the lifestyle of a true kingdom apostolic community people, according to the book of Acts.

"Then they that gladly received his word were baptized: and the same day there were added unto them about three thousand souls. And they continued stedfastly in the apostles' doctrine and fellowship, and in breaking of bread, and in prayers. And fear came upon every soul: and many wonders and signs were done by the apostles. And all that believed were together, and had all things common; And sold their possessions and goods, and parted them to all men, as every man had need. And they, continuing daily with one accord in the temple, and breaking bread from house to house, did eat their meat with gladness and singleness of heart, Praising God, and having favour with all the people. And the Lord added to the Church daily such as should be saved" - (Acts 2:41-47).

1. They received the word and were baptized in the name of Jesus into the Body of Christ.

Baptism is almost a lost experience within most of the churches today. It has been taught to be a kind of religious ritual, and the people have lost the primary focus of this experience, and how it relates to our salvation to become born again into the kingdom of God.

Baptism in the name of the Lord Jesus is a foundational principle and experience that brings us into union with Jesus, and His Body (Christ). Baptism releases us into an incorruptible life in Christ - a walk in newness of life (Romans 6:3-9). Our reaction to the eternal word of God compels us into a public proclamation of our union with the Word, which is Christ. This is the experience that confirms and guarantees our salvation. We must be born of water (Water Baptism) and of the Spirit (Holy Spirit Baptism) to enter into the kingdom of God.

"Jesus answered and said unto him, Verily, verily, I say unto thee, Except a man be born again, he cannot see the kingdom of God. Nicodemus saith unto Him, How can a man be born when he is old? can he enter the second time into his mother's womb, and be born? Jesus answered, Verily, verily, I say unto thee, Except a man be born of water and of the Spirit, he cannot enter into the kingdom of God" - (John 3:3-5).

The pattern of the apostles in the early Church in the New Testament was that they preached Jesus, revealing to the people that He is the Christ the Messiah that is to come as prophesied in the scriptures, and as they believed the word that is preached and accepted Christ's finished works, they were immediately baptptized in water and Spirit - Acts 10:34-48.

"But when they believed Philip preaching the things concerning the kingdom of God, and the name of Jesus Christ, they were baptized, both men and women" - (Acts 8:12).

There are so many contentions on how water baptism is done. Should it be done "in the name of the Father, and the Son, and the Holy Spirit"? Or "in the Name of Jesus Christ"? This has brought much contention and division within the Body of Christ.

Matthew 28:19 - 'Baptizing them in the name of the Father, the Son and the Holy Ghost' stands alone as the only scripture to that way. And ONE scripture alone does not make a doctrine or set a standard, there has to be one or more scriptures that bear witness to the truth.

The pattern observed in the book of Acts which is frequently seen or done by the apostles is, "Baptizing them in the Name of Jesus Christ". This ofcourse is the New Testament pattern.

However, I love the way a dear brother puts it; "I baptize you in the name of the Father and of the Son, and the Holy Spirit in Jesus Christ Name". Amen. That settles it, instead of creating divisions among ourselves. Selah!

2. They devoted themselves continually to the apostles' doctrine (teachings of the Lord Jesus Christ).

Paul the apostle made a significant statement in his prayer for the Church in Ephesus for them to comprehend the eternal pupose of God in Christ (Ephesians 1:15-23). His desire was that God would impart to them the Spirit of wisdom and the revelation of the knowledge of Him (Christ), because Jesus is the express image of God's person to mankind, and our knowledge of Him is our knowledge of the Father. To know Jesus is to know the Father. To have an intimate relationship with Jesus is to have an intimate relationship with the Father, because Jesus is God's self revelation to us.

The apostles' doctrine is primarily the teachings of the Lord Jesus Christ as revealed to them through their personal walk with Him. The early Church did not have the New Testament epistles because it was not written then; and they obviously weren't teaching the law. All they knew was the teachings of Jesus which are recorded in the four gospels according to the books of Matthew, Mark, Luke and John. The only reference to the Old Testament was to reveal Christ (The Messiah) to them as prophetically spoken, and to show to the people that Jesus is the Messiah.

The true doctrinal foundation of the apostles and prophets was the basic fundamental doctrines of Christ in Hebrews 6:1-2, which they were established upon, and beyond that, they continued to grow up in Christ, and in the deeper things of God.

If we must build accurately according to the divine pattern of God, then Jesus Christ must be the foundation and the center of our message; and not ourselves, not made-made traditions, not prosperity, not miracles nor breakthroughs.

3. There is an ongoing fellowship with the Body of Christ.

The purpose of fellowship is to receive mutual impartation

from the different measure of grace the Lord has given to the Body in order to fulfill our assignment. Every believer must be able to draw strength from the Christ that is within the fellowship. The time and place of fellowship is not about spiritual entertainment. True fellowship should bring us beyond the soul realm (Outer Court) into the Spirit realm (Most Holy Place) where Christ is ALL.

"We should not stop gathering together (fellowshipping) with other believers, as some of you are doing. Instead, we must continue to encourage each other even more as we see the day of the Lord coming" - (Hebrews 10:25 GW).

4. There is a commitment to the breaking of bread (communion) from house to house.

Communion is not a religious sacrament that is taken by the church on special occasions, but it is the expression of our identification with Christ, and the proclamation of the finished works of Christ. This is the essence of our faith in Him - His death, burial and resurrection (1 Corinthians 11:23-26; 15:12-20).

Communion is the gift of God's love and grace given to humanity in Christ, because by the brokenness of His Body we have wholeness, and by the pouring of His blood He sanctified and redeemed us.

Communion should become a daily practice and part of our spiritual living, not only at ocassional Church fellowship, but within the family table at home, and every time the saints come together for fellowship. '*For as often as we do this, in remembrance of the Lord Jesus, we do show the Lord's death till He come*' - 1 Corinthians 11:23-26.

5. They were fervent and keen in prayers.

Fervent prayers must become our driving force. The Church is called to be a house of prayer for all nations. We must not underestimate the power of corporate prayers when the Church unites to pray.

"....for mine house shall be called an house of prayer for all people" - (Isaiah 56:7).

"And the LORD appeared to Solomon by night, and said unto him, I have heard thy prayer, and have chosen this place to myself for an house of sacrifice. If I shut up heaven that there be no rain, or if I command the locusts to devour the land, or if I send pestilence among my people; If my people, which are called by my name, shall humble themselves, and pray, and seek my face, and turn from their wicked ways; then will I hear from heaven, and will forgive their sin, and will heal their land. Now mine eyes shall be open, and mine ears attent unto the prayer that is made in this place. For now have I chosen and sanctified this house, that my name may be there for ever: and mine eyes and mine heart shall be there perpetually" - (2 Chronicles 7:12-16).

"After this manner therefore pray ye: Our Father which art in heaven, Hallowed be thy name. Thy kingdom come. Thy will be done in earth, as it is in heaven. Give us this day our daily bread" - (Matthew 6:9-11).

Prayer is not about our desire and needs being met, but it is about God's will being established on earth. Out of the establishment of His will, there is a supply for our needs - Matthew 6:33.

The key to releasing the kingdom of God on earth is prayer. The lost art of prayer must be restored back to the Church if His kingdom must be established, and if we want to see a change in every sphere of our lives and community. A praying Church is a prevailing Church. If there is a Church to pray, there is a God to answer.

6. They walked in the fear of God and in reverence.

The fear of God is not dreadfulness or the spirit of fear that brings oppression and bondage, but it is the awe acknowledgement of God's divinity that compels one to total obedience and submission to His will. It is the feeling of reverential respect combined with wonder. **God has not given us the spirit of fear** (2 Timothy 1:7).

The fear of God will bring us to our knees before Him in the secret place. The fear of God will keep us from the sins that rob us of His glory and anointing. The fear of God will condition our heart to the ways of God. It will cause us to reverence God in complete obedience to His commandment.

The absence of the fear of God will create an attitude and a desire not to seek the way of the knowledge of God. This was the case with the men that was brought to dwell in Samaria by the king of Assyria after the people of Israel was carried away out of Samaria. These men did not know the customs and manner of God because they lacked the fear of God. So the Lord sent lions among them, which killed some of them.

A priest had to be sent to teach them how they should fear the Lord so they can be delivered from destruction.

"And so it was at the beginning of their dwelling there, that they feared not the LORD: therefore the LORD sent lions among them, which slew some of them. Wherefore they spake to the king of Assyria, saying, The nations which thou hast removed, and placed in the cities of Samaria, know not the manner of the God of the land: therefore he hath sent lions among them, and, behold, they slay them, because they know not the manner of the God of the land. Then the king of Assyria commanded, saying, Carry thither one of the priests whom ye brought from thence; and let them go and dwell there, and let him teach them the manner of the God of the land. Then one of the priests whom they had carried away from Samaria came and dwelt in Bethel, and taught them how they should fear the LORD" - (2 Kings 17:25-28).

The Church of today lacks the respect and fear of God. There is no law and order as people cast off restraint, hence there is no desire to know and follow the custom and the laws of the Lord. The fear of God is needed in the Body of Christ today for us to walk in order and reverence. This will help us to know the customs and manner of God and walk in His way.

"Let us hear the conclusion of the whole matter: Fear God, and keep His commandments: for this is the whole duty of man" - (Ecclesiastes 12:13).

7. There are <u>signs and wonders</u> among the people.

"Through mighty signs and wonders, by the power of the Spirit of God; so that from Jerusalem, and round about unto Illyricum, I have fully preached the gospel of Christ" - (Romans 15:19).

"And my speech and my preaching was not with enticing

words of man's wisdom, but in demonstration of the Spirit and of power: That your faith should not stand in the wisdom of men, but in the power of God" - (1 Corinthians 2:4-5).

"Truly the signs of an apostle were wrought among you in all patience, in signs, and wonders, and mighty deeds" - (1 Corinthians 12:12).

Signs and wonders are a mark of an apostolic people (Church). We cannot present a powerless gospel to the world and expect them to believe in Jesus Christ. The Church must go beyond the eloquence of the enticing words of man's wisdom, and manifest the power of the Spirit of God.

"A powerless Gospel is only propaganda, promotion or business church growth. Without the Holy Spirit we dress the shop window without having the goods on the shelves. 'Be filled with the Spirit' is an ultimatum not an ultimate aim; an initial necessity and not a final achievement" - Reinhard Bonnke.

The Church of the Lord Jesus Christ is a Church of Power, Signs and Wonders.

"The power of God shows us that God is not a fairy tale for grown-ups but a wonderful reality. Without the power of God our faith is empty. If all we have is theory, philosophy, theology and other intellectual arguments, we will never have a faith that changes the world. God is not a theory, He is real, He is full of life and power" - God Is Real Today.

As we build all things according to the pattern of God and His divine order, we must go to the prayer closet and tarry on our knees until we are fully endued with the power of the Holy

Spirit from on high.

8. They walked in love with one another and there is provision to meet needs.

Love is more than a deep affection or feeling that we have for one another. Love is an expression of who God is. Love is the character of God. A true Church is an expression of who God is here on earth. The Church must therefore express love, because that is who God is.

The significance of our life is NOT measured by the abundance of things we possess, but by the impact we make in our generation and in the next through our action of love for one another. We must always remember that 'a person's life doesn't consist of the amount of possessions he has' - Luke 12:15.

Love is selfless and sacrificial. True love is to give or make sacrifice without any expectation. We must be sacrificial in our attitude and relationship with one another in the Church to share what we have to help meet the needs of others. We cannot love without giving.

Love is the sum of all things in Christ - 1 Corinthians 13:1-13.

The expression of our love for God, which is correlated to our love for one another, is a reflection of our knowledge of Him rooted in our relationship with Him, placing us in a position where we are now also known of Him.

"Beloved, let us love one another: for love is of God; and every one that loveth is born of God, and knoweth God. He that loveth not knoweth not God; for God is love" - (1 John 4:7-8).

Love is fundamental to our faith, and it is a powerful force that can change anything.

9. They were walking in oneness (unity).

The prayer and desire of Jesus is that we be united as ONE. We cannot neglect the fact that there is power and blessings in unity. The Church must be united. The Church must be ONE. It is our responsibility to pursue after this desire of the Father to walk in oneness.

"Neither pray I for these alone, but for them also which shall believe on me through their word; That they all may be one; as thou, Father, art in me, and I in thee, that they also may be one in us: that the world may believe that thou hast sent me. And the glory which thou gavest me I have given them; that they may be one, even as we are one: I in them, and thou in me, that they may be made perfect in one; and that the world may know that thou hast sent me, and hast loved them, as thou hast loved me" - (John 17:20-23).

"Endeavouring to keep the unity of the Spirit in the bond of peace. There is one body, and one Spirit, even as ye are called in one hope of your calling; One Lord, one faith, one baptism, One God and Father of all, who is above all, and through all, and in you all" - Ephesians 4:3-6).

We cannot be one with the Father and with Christ, and be divided with the saints. Our oneness with the Father is manifested in our oneness with His Body - His Church.

"Behold, how good and how pleasant it is for brethren to dwell together in unity! It is like the precious ointment upon the head, that ran down upon the beard, even Aaron's beard: that went down to the skirts of his garments; As the dew of Hermon, and as the dew that descended upon the mountains of Zion: for there the LORD commanded the blessing, even life for evermore" - (Psalm 133:1-3).

"That ye may with one mind and one mouth glorify God, even the Father of our Lord Jesus Christ. Wherefore receive ye one another, as Christ also received us to the glory of God" - (Romans 15:6-7).

10. There is gladness and sincerity of heart.

"Every day they continued to meet together in the temple courts. They broke bread in their homes and ate together with glad and sincere hearts" - (Acts 2:46 NIV).

This is a true picture of genuine spiritual fellowship - every man worthy of the confidence of his brother; and all walking by the same rule, and minding the same thing.

Sincerity of heart implies that there is absence of pretence, deceit or hypocrisy. We must desire at all cost to walk with God and with our brothers/sisters with an unquestionable character - a sincere heart.

"Therefore seeing we have this ministry, as we have received mercy, we faint not; But have renounced the hidden things of dishonesty, not walking in craftiness, nor handling the word of God deceitfully; but by manifestation of the truth commending ourselves to every man's conscience in the sight of God" - (2 Corinthians 4:1-2).

Our ministry must be that of integrity and truthfulness. People should be able to find us trustworthy and be glad to break bread with us with a free heart.

"These are the things that ye shall do; Speak ye every man the truth to his neighbour; execute the judgment of truth and peace in your gates: And let none of you imagine evil in your hearts against his neighbour; and love no false oath: for all these are things that I hate, saith the LORD" - (Zechariah 8:16-17).

11. They have an attitude of praise unto God.

Praise is an attitude of gratitude. Praise is expressed not in the heart, but through our lips. Praise is the fruit of the lips, but a product of the heart.

"By Him therefore let us offer the sacrifice of praise to God continually, that is, the fruit of our lips giving thanks to His name" - (Hebrews 13:15).

"Praise affects you, it affects the devil, and it affects God. It touches everything and every part of your life. Likewise, a lack of praise affects you in a negative way, turns the devil loose in your life, and doesn't bless God. You have to get this area of your life right " - Andrew Wommack.

12. They walked in favour with all the people.

One of the marks of Christ upon His Church is FAVOUR. As we develop our relationship with Christ and the saints and grow in the deeper things of the Lord, He gives us the ability to walk in favour with all the people.

When there is a genuine community spirit among the Church, the Lord begins to move the hearts of people to look upon us with favour.

The blessing of the Lord is favour - unlimited grace.

13. There is an increase of souls into the Body on a daily basis.

"......the Lord added to their number day by day those who were being saved" - (Acts 2:47).

Numerical increase in the Church does not come through programs or application of principles; it comes only from the Lord. It is the Lord that gives increase. It is the Lord that does the adding to His Church.

"I have planted, Apollos watered; but God gave the increase. So then neither is he that planteth any thing, neither he that watereth; **but God that giveth the increase**" - (1 Corinthians 3:6-7).

When we are obedient to make all things according to the pattern of God, *He will give us the increase*. It is not man's strength or strategy, but it is of His grace. This grace is a daily load. Day by day He added to the Church. Hallelujah!

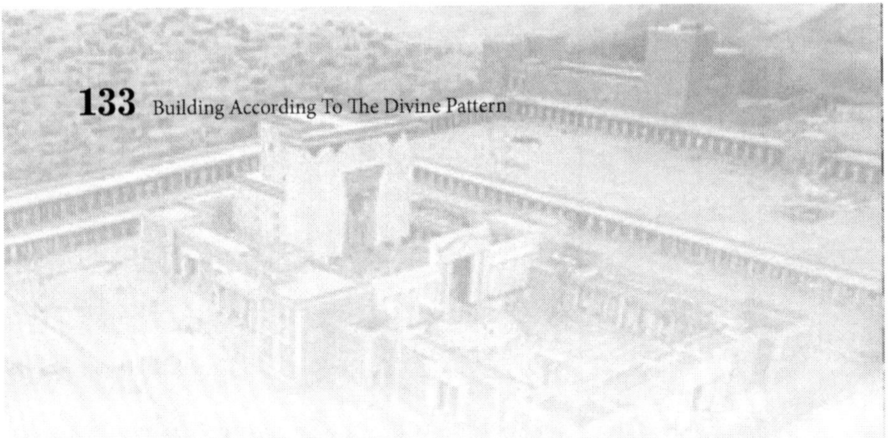

The Seven Mountains of Influence

"Governmental Churches - Agent Of Change And Transformation"

"It will come about in the last days that the mountain that is the LORD's Temple will be established as the highest of mountains, it will be raised above the hills; all the nations will stream to it. Many groups of people will come, commenting, "Come! Let's go up to the Temple of the God of Jacob that they may teach us His ways. Then let's walk in His paths." - (Isaiah 2:2-3).

Chapter Nine

The Seven Mountains of Influence

In advancing the kingdom of God we are to influence the earth for Christ. The Church must be a positive agent of change and transformation in the community. We are a Governmental Church. The saints must rise and take their place in society as God's agent.

There is what is known today as the Seven Mountains of Influence, and the nations of the earth are changed and transformed through these Seven Mountains.

1. Family
2. Religion - (Spirituality)
3. Business - (Economy, Finance)
4. Politics - (Government)
5. Education
6. Media - (Communication)
7. Arts - (Entertainment, Celebration, Sports)

These Seven Mountains of Influence are considered to be cultures that mould the way we think and they influences our lives on a daily basis. If we are to make any significant impact and change in the community as a Church, we must engage these Seven Mountains of societal spheres and influence them for Christ and His kingdom. By so doing we can bring change and transformation to a nation.

"Tell him this is what the LORD Almighty says: 'Here is the man whose name is the Branch, and he will branch out from his place and build the temple of the LORD.

It is he who will build the temple of the LORD, and he will be clothed with majesty and will sit and rule on his throne. And he will be a priest on his throne. And there will be harmony between the two" - (Zachariah 6:12-13 NIV).

"You let them become kings and serve God as priests, and they will rule on earth" - (Revelation 5:10 CEV).

The priesthood is your ministry to God, and His people, but the kingship is the administration of God's government and authority in you, and through you in the market-place and in these mountains. There has to be a balance and co-existence of harmony between both offices/ministries in order to build the house of God. We must assume our role as priests and take our place on the throne as kings to rule. The priest will sit on the throne as king - (We are priests in the ministry, and kings in the market-places).

From a spiritual point of view, mountain(s) are considered to be government, authority, ruler-ship, principalities, dominion and a place or position of influence.

The strategy for the Church to be able to influence these spheres (Seven Mountains) and bring transformation to our society is through the marketplace (workplace). Because ninety percent (90%) of our time is spent in these spheres and if we can build and equip the saints to take their positions in society, and see their workplace as part of their God given assignment, then the Church can begin to positively influence these spheres and occupy places as the principles of the kingdom are being released.

This is not something that can be done by one person or one local fellowship in a twinkling of an eye. It will take a process of time, but it requires revelation and understanding for the involvement of a corporate people with a kingdom mindset to engage these seven spheres.

(1) Family.

A family is a fundamental group typically consisting of two parents (father and mother) or more people (children inclusive) who are the vital organs sharing the same goals and values and having long-term commitments to one another and usually residing in the same dwelling place. This is an inclusive concept of masculine and feminine - father, mother, sons and daughters. The family is the first institution established by God through the covenant of marriage. One of His aims was that the family grows to become a peculiar tribe of people who are separated to be His treasured possession.

"We are a people holy to the LORD your God. The LORD your God has chosen you to be a people for His treasured possession, out of all the peoples who are on the face of the earth. It was not because you were more in number than any other people that the LORD set His love on you and chose you, for you were the fewest of all peoples, but it is because the LORD loves you...." - (Deuteronomy 7:6 -8 ESV).

The order of God's dealing with creation, and the administration of His purposes in the earth is first with an individual through whom He establishes a family, and that family becomes the corporate body that He uses to impact the nations – the earth realm, to establish His purpose. This is clearly seen in the promise to the patriarch Abraham as it relates to his family and the nations.

"Now the LORD had said unto Abram, ...I will make of thee a great nation, and I will bless thee, and make thy name great; and thou shalt be a blessing.....and in thee shall all families of the earth be blessed" – (Genesis 12:1-3).

"The LORD said to Himself, "I should tell Abraham what I am going to do, since his family will become a great and powerful nation that will be a blessing to all other nations on earth." – (Genesis 18:17-18 CEV).

The promise of God to Abraham was so weighty, yet his greatness and the fulfillment was not in himself, but in his seed (Son), to whom the promise was given and who becomes the instrument of releasing God's fullness and blessings upon the earth.

"Behold, I will send you Elijah the prophet before the coming of the great and dreadful day of the LORD. And he shall turn the heart of the fathers to the children, and the heart of the children to their fathers, lest I come and smite the earth with a curse" - (Malachi 4:5-6).

Family is of important interest to God. His aim is to restore families, and this will break the curse of fatherlessness that is upon the nations.

The devil knows this that is why there has been an intensive attack against the original institution of marriage (man and woman) and against the family at large. Divorce and same sex relationships and all forms of family abuse are all strategies of the enemy to destroy the family.

The Church must have a clear understanding of this and become involved in the restoration of the values of godly families, so we can empower the saints through an exemplary lifestyle and raising strong families that will boldly influence this mountain of family. ***Let us model Christ in the family.***

Our influence in the society is greatly dependent on the influence of the family values that are instilled in us. When men rise to become true fathers and women rise to become true mothers to protect and establish godly values it will cause us to measure up to something.

(2) Religion - (Spirituality).

Religion has been defined as a collection of cultural systems, beliefs, and world views that establishes symbols relating humanity to spirituality and sometimes to moral values.

Religion has often been said to be man's way of attempting to reach God, and is rooted in external works (human efforts). The Church is not a religion rooted in external works, but it is a relationship based on faith, and is an internal attitude (Christ's works). It is God's way reaching out to mankind through relationship with Jesus Christ. What really matters is for people to be in right relationship with God, and to let this be the primary purpose of their lives.

"Faithful is the God by whom you were called into fellowship with His Son Jesus the Messiah, our Lord" - (1Corinthians 1:9 CEV).

"For it pleased the Father that in Him (Jesus) should all fulness dwell; And, having made peace through the blood of His cross, by Him (Jesus) to reconcile all things unto Himself; by Him (Jesus), I say,whether they be things in earth, or things in heaven.

And you, that were sometime alienated and enemies in your mind by wicked works, yet now hath He reconciled" - (Colossians 1:19-21).

The word "Christians" has never been the original intent of the name given by God to the early disciples and the apostles of Jesus Christ to define who they were in their relationship with Him. The name "Christians" was first given to them by the Gentiles and religious sects who were in Antioch, an ancient Greek city.

".....And the disciples were called Christians first in Antioch" - (Acts 11:26).

The early disciples and apostles of Jesus Christ were originally known as people of the way (*Followers of the Way of Christ*) - John 14:6, Acts 9:2; Acts 19:8-9, 23; Acts 22:4; Acts 24:22.

In the sight of God, our Father, we are known and called 'sons of God'.

"But as many as did receive Him (Jesus) to them He gave authority to become sons of God—to those believing in His name (Jesus)" - (John 1:12 YLT).

"For as many as are led by the Spirit of God, they are the sons of God" - (Romans 8:14).

"But when the fulness of the time was come, God sent forth His Son, made of a woman, made under the law, To redeem them that were under the law, that we might receive the adoption of sons. And because ye are sons, God hath sent forth the Spirit of His Son into your hearts, crying, Abba, Father.

Wherefore thou art no more a servant, but a son; and if a son, then an heir of God through Christ" - (Galatians 4:4-7).

"Behold, what manner of love the Father hath bestowed upon us, that we should be called the sons of God: therefore the world knoweth us not, because it knew Him not. Beloved, now are we the sons of God, and it doth not yet appear what we shall be: but we know that, when He (Jesus) shall appear, we shall be like Him (Jesus); for we shall see Him (Jesus) as He (Jesus) is" - (1 John 3:1-2).

The world has called us Christians and defined us as a religion based on their belief system that is rooted in humanism. They have no knowledge of Christ, hence they don't know us.

Christianity (if I may use this word for the sake of this book) is considered to be a religion based on the world's perspective; but in its purest form, ***our spirituality is NOT a religion.*** If there be any form of religion (human effort) to be reckoned with our spirituality which is undefiled to God, our Father, it is, *"to visit the fatherless and widows in their affliction, and to keep oneself unspotted from the world"* - James 1:27.

In our modern era, religion has become a mountain that governs many aspects of human existence, and it has been implicated in all sorts of conflict and violence globally. We cannot deny the fact that we have not been affected by the effects of religion, either positively or negatively. There is a present awakening of religion among the nations considering the violent activities of terrorism and human barbarism that is done in the name of religion.

Our spirituality must therefore influence this mountain of religion to shape the mindset of humanity through a righteous judgment of peace, because we are a mountain called by God to be a spiritual government over all the mountains.

Zion is a mountain. Zion is God's dwelling place. We (the Church) are the dwelling place of God. We are His tabernacle. We are Zion. We are a mountain!

"His abode has been established in Salem, His dwelling place in Zion" - (Psalm 76:2 ESV).

"For the LORD hath chosen Zion; He hath desired it for His habitation. This is my rest for ever: here will I dwell; for I have desired it" - (Psalm 132:113-14).

"The LORD said unto my Lord, Sit thou at my right hand, until I make thine enemies thy footstool. The LORD shall send the rod of thy strength out of Zion: rule thou in the midst of thine enemies" - (Psalm 110:1-2).

Zion is the governmental seat of God - place of ruler-ship. Zion is God's habitation (God's House - His Church) established on the mountain above the hills from where His laws shall proceed to rule the nations.

"So shall ye know that I am the LORD your God dwelling in Zion, my holy mountain: then shall Jerusalem be holy, and there shall no strangers pass through her any more. And it shall come to pass in that day, that the mountains shall drop down new wine, and the hills shall flow with milk, and all the rivers of Judah shall flow with waters, and a fountain shall come forth of the house of the LORD, and shall water the valley of Shittim" - (Joel 3:17-18).

"But in the last days it shall come to pass, that the mountain of the house of the LORD shall be established in the top of the mountains, and it shall be exalted above the hills; and people shall flow unto it. And many nations shall come, and say, Come, and let us go up to the mountain of the LORD, and to the house of the God of Jacob; and He will teach us of His ways, and we will walk in His paths: for the law shall go forth of Zion, and the word of the LORD from Jerusalem" - (Micah 4:1-2).

"For this Agar is mount Sinai in Arabia, and answereth to Jerusalem which now is, and is in bondage with her children. But Jerusalem which is above is free, which is the mother of us all" - (Galatians 4:25-26).

In consideration of the above scriptures referencing Jerusalem, it is important to note that Galatians Chapter 4 makes it clear that there are two Jerusalems. The first one is referred to as the physical Jerusalem in the Middle East which now is, and is in bondage with her children.

We are not of the first Jerusalem. We are of the second Jerusalem which is above and free, which is the mother of us all. This second Jerusalem is the holy city, the great city of God, the new heavenly Jerusalem.

"But ye are come unto mount Sion, and unto the city of the living God, the heavenly Jerusalem, and to an innumerable company of angels, To the general assembly and church of the firstborn, which are written in heaven, and to God the Judge of all, and to the spirits of just men made perfect" - (Hebrews 12:22-23).

"Him that overcometh will I make a pillar in the temple of my God, and he shall go no more out: and I will write upon him the name of my God, and the name of the city of my God, which is new Jerusalem, which cometh down out of heaven from my God: and I will write upon him my new name" - (Revelation 3:12).

"And I John saw the holy city, new Jerusalem, coming down from God out of heaven, prepared as a bride adorned for her husband....And there came unto me one of the seven angels which had the seven vials full of the seven last plagues, and talked with me, saying, Come hither, I will shew thee the bride, the Lamb's wife. And he carried me away in the spirit to a great and high mountain, and shewed me that great city, the holy Jerusalem, descending out of heaven from God" - (Revelation 21:2, 9-10).

Interestingly, the angel of the Lord said to John, come let me show you the bride, the Lamb's wife. You would expect that the angel will show John a woman, because the bride must be a person, but rather, the angel carried John away in the spirit to a great and high mountain and showed him a place, that great city, the holy Jerusalem, descending out of heaven from God.

The bride, the Lamb's wife is *NOT* a place, but a *Person*; and here this Person is defined with the characteristics as that great city, the holy Jerusalem, descending out of heaven from God. This in itself changes the whole perception *from a place to a person* - (a corporate people in Christ that is the Body of Christ).

The Church is the bride, the Lamb's wife. The Body of Christ/ Bride consists of those who have confessed and received Jesus Christ as their Lord and personal savior, and have received eternal life. Christ, the Bridegroom, has chosen the Body of Christ (the Church) to be His bride sacrificially and lovingly - (Ephesians 5:25-27, 2 Corinthians 11:2).

Let us be an example and a true expression of the Body of Christ as we build accurately and influence this mountain of religion, as it has been prophetically spoken that we will be the mountain on top of all mountains. Our spirituality must make an impact among other religions, and this is only when we declare the gospel of he kingdom of God.

(3) Business - (Economy, Finance).

One of the challenges we have encountered as a Body has been the ignorance that prevails within the Church regarding 'kingdom economics'. The global elite govern the world with the strategy of controlling every financial institution and enslaving us with debts through our mortgages, bonds, loans etc. Their goal is also to enslave governments as they finance political campaigns; and in controlling governments, the whole nation are enslaved.

But we have a heavenly system that is not of this world, which gives us unreserved access into the supernatural economy of God that prevails above all other economies and systems, allowing us to live in peace and prosperity. The challenge here is that we don't know how to access the economy of God, or we are not accessing it to the fullness of God's potential for us. This has resulted to a beggarly mentality that continues to enslave the Church and rob us of our destiny and the actualization of our assignment on earth.

"..... For the children of this world are in their generation wiser than the children of light" - (Luke 16:8).

The parable of the dishonest manager was the fact that he knew how to manipulate his system to profit his own interest against the day of his adversity, and his lord commended him - Luke 16:1-12.

The problem with the Church is that we are not raising faithful stewards, hence the true riches are not entrusted to us. We are found wanting! The children of this world are said to be wiser than the children of light, because they know that we have a system from above which is in a higher order that supersedes theirs, but we have left this higher order and seek to operate with their worldly system which is of no profit to our assignment. We cannot apply the system of this world and expect a supernatural result.

Over the years there have been prophetic declarations of Isaiah 60:1-7, about the transfer of wealth, and the camels which are coming with kings riding upon them with treasures of the earth. As much as this is true, the reality is that the mountains of business, finance, economy etc will not be influenced by the Church if we only prophesy, pray and then sit down. **There has to be a strategic development of Joseph's technology and mindset to train, equip and empower the saints with this grace to engage this mountain of business (Finance, Economy).** A whole new generation of kingdom leaders and saints must be raised up in the market-place and the economic world that will strategically develop godly principles to influence and occupy this mountain.

Joseph the Jewish lad who was sold as a slave by his brothers was made the governor over the land of Egypt - Genesis 42:6.

He controlled the economy of Egypt in the midst of famine and opened the storehouses to the nations, preserving the heritage of God's people and bringing unity among his brothers. In the midst of challenges, he went through the process of development to make his dream a reality. From his lowest position in the pit and in prison he rose to occupy a seat in the king's palace in a foreign land. He gained favour with God and with those in authority.

"And they went up out of Egypt, and came into the land of Canaan unto Jacob their father, And told him, saying, Joseph is yet alive, and he is governor over all the land of Egypt. And Jacob's heart fainted, for he believed them not. And they told him all the words of Joseph, which he had said unto them: and when he saw the wagons which Joseph had sent to carry him, the spirit of Jacob their father revived: And Israel said, It is enough; Joseph my son is yet alive: I will go and see him before I die" - (Genesis 45:25-28).

This question stands before us today; where are the Josephs of our day who will administrate and be in command of the economy?

This must be a corporate effort of the Body and not just an individual. The Church must learn to work together in unity and as a team to achieve this goal of ruling in the economic mountain.

"The LORD shall command the blessing upon thee in thy storehouses, and in all that thou settest thine hand unto; and He shall bless thee in the land which the LORD thy God giveth thee" - (Deuteronomy 28:8).

It is time to set our hand to business, and the Lord shall bless us in the land to rule on this mountain.

(4) Politics - (Government).

The truth remains that the Church must change her perspective regarding politics and government, or we will become irrelevant in today's world.

"When the [uncompromisingly] righteous are in authority, the people rejoice; but when the wicked man rules, the people groan and sigh" - (Proverbs 29:2 Amplified Bible).

"Then God blessed them and said, "Be fruitful and multiply. Fill the earth and **govern it.** Reign over the fish in the sea, the birds in the sky, and all the animals that scurry along the ground" - (Genesis 1:28).

<u>God's purpose for our dominion mandate is not to rule over humans, but over the creation order</u>. We are authorized by God to maintain order in the earth. The desire to rule over other people is from man's fallen nature, and this continues to be the driving force behind our present day government as the people are being controlled and exploited for personal gains.

The fundamental purpose of government is supposed to be the maintenance of basic order and to provide a system in which every individual has the liberty to access basic human rights with equality in line with God's will and principles. When this is uncompromised in government then the people will rejoice.

The question is, how can the righteous be in authority when they are not involved in politics or government?

If we cannot train and position the saints in places of influence and governmental authority then the wicked will continue to rule and we will be subject to the ridicules of the enemy and unlawful decisions that will be established, even to the detriment of our faith. This is without doubt, as we can see among the nations instituting and legalizing homosexual 'rights' and how the Church is being forced to compromise its belief in God's word against this abominable act.

When Haman stood as an enemy against the Jews and plotted to destroy them, nothing would have been able to avert the destruction that was coming if Queen Esther had not stood in the king's inner court to mediate for salvation - Esther 4:10-17. She desecrated the laws of the king's palace and stepped into the inner court to meet with the king declaring "*...if I perish, I perish*". The only reason Esther stood in this position was because she was prepared by Mordecai to take it, even though she was a Jew and it was not her right to do so. Mordecai recognized that she was prepared in her royal position *for such a time as this.*

This question stands before us today; have we as a Church prepared our Esther's that will stand in the place of governmental authorities for times such as this?

(5) Education.

The importance of education and the role it plays in the development of human character, and the influence it has on our world cannot be overemphasized, because this is the premise that forms the very essence of all our actions. What we do and become is what we know and have learned. Education is a self-enlightening process. It leads to enlightenment, either spiritually or physically.

"The direction in which education starts a man will determine his future in life" - Plato.

Another important aspect of education is that it is very crucial to the whole development of man and it helps to shape and build our character.

"The function of education is to teach one to think intensively and to think critically. Intelligence plus character - that is the goal of true education" - Martin Luther King, Jr.

"Education is the most powerful weapon we can use to change the world" - Nelson Mandela.

Education provides us with knowledge about our world. It lays the foundation for a stronger nation, because education is the brain of a nation.

The day a man stops to learn is the day he starts to die. Education is life, but the question is, what are we being educated in?

Drug abuse, gangsters, prostitution, crime, unemployment and most barbaric actions are tied to the lack of proper godly education which has shaped the mindset of our generation.

"Education is simply the soul of a society as it passes from one generation to another" - G. K. Chesterton.

We cannot deny the fact that education shapes the mind of many generations as it influences their behavior and what they become.

This therefore makes the mountain of education an important

sphere that we must influence to be able to dominate and rule. It begins from the basis - the family!

(6) Media - (Communication).

The Media is the main means of mass communication reaching a large audience, whether written, broadcast or spoken - (television, radio, newspapers, magazines, internet, movies and advertisements and so forth). It is a significant force that has the capacity to create the cultures that always influences and defines the character of a people geographically. The media is a stronghold that influences and controls the minds of people.

The works of darkness, illuminati, baphomet, wickedness, idolatry, heresies, sexual immoralities and abominable acts, such as gay marriages, lesbianism and witchcraft is being widely promoted and accepted as normal culture, and even praised and glamorized on movies, television, social medias and so forth.

"Wherein in time past ye walked according to the course of this world, according to the prince of the power of the air, the spirit that now worketh in the children of disobedience" - (Ephesians 2:2).

Media is air-(waves) and it is a spirit. Air is symbolic of the spirit. Satan is known as the prince of the power of the air (media), the spirit that controls people to make them walk in disobedience. Satan is a ruler and authority of the air - airwaves.

The media continues to be the platform to promote the dark side of the kingdom of darkness and to keep people captive to the course of this world.

"While the women went on their way, some of the soldiers guarding the tomb went back to the city and told the chief priests everything that had happened. **The chief priests met with the elders and made their plan; they gave a large sum of money to the soldiers and said, "You are to say that His disciples came during the night and stole His body while you were asleep**. And if the Governor should hear of this, we will convince him that you are innocent, and you will have nothing to worry about." **The guards took the money and did what they were told to do. And so that is the report spread around by the Jews to this very day**" - (Matthew 28:11-15 GNT).

The chief priests and the religious sects took counsel and gave a large sum of money as bribe to the soldiers, which is sufficient to propagate a false report until this day, to deny the truth about Jesus Christ our Lord and Savior who arose from the dead on the third day, and is alive.

Billions of dollars is invested in media to control the air-waves to propagate lies and false reports, because anything that can be on the media will be accepted by the people and sold to them.

Does it matter to us as a Church that this mountain of media and communication is also available to us in many ways and we can influence this mountain through a large sum of money if we invest to propagate the gospel of the kingdom of God through the right channels? The enemy is investing a large sum of money to promote lies and their agenda, but we as the Church is holding back and doing nothing.

Truth is costly. The cost of discipleship to advance the kingdom of God on earth will cost us everything. If we are not willing to give up all for the truth, then we are not worth to be called a disciple of the Lord Jesus Christ.

Why do we waste our energy and time fighting against one another on the media and give ourselves to foolishness, when we can utilize that platform and channel our energy for Christ and His kingdom!

(7). Arts - (Entertainment, Celebration, Music, Sports etc).

To many, Arts - (Entertainment, Sports, Music etc) has become an idol that has captivated many hearts, influencing behavior and attitude towards one another.

Youths and adults alike are influenced by the music industry. It plays into the soul, and it can open people to a certain dimension and realm of influence and control in their spirit.

I believe as a Church we need to explore this mountain and be creative to release a pure Spirit.

If there is anything that is needed to fulfill this mandate, it is GRACE. It will take the grace of God for a people to walk in this place and position, and to finish this work and make a significant impact for the Lord and His kingdom.

The Spirit of grace is being poured out upon the Church. Great grace is given to enable us as we labour in the market-place. There is no limit to what the grace of God will do as He makes the impossible become possible.

"Who are you, O great mountain, before Zerubbabel you shall become a plain! And he shall bring forth the capstone with shouts of "Grace, grace to it!" - (Zachariah 4:7).

The capstone is a ministry with a finishing mentality. There is a capstone ministry that is a finishing anointing that operates with the grace of God to overcome and finish God's purpose. This capstone - finishing ministry will shout Grace, Grace to it.

When we shift focus from only revelation knowledge acquisition to implementation of revelation knowledge then we can begin to see a transformation in these mountains and raise creative and empowered kingdom dominion citizens who are ruling and influencing their world for Christ.

God has given us a governmental authority. Let us therefore take our place and position. Let's be His government upon these mountains by His grace, and let His kingdom come and let His will be done on earth as it is in heaven.

International Training & Resource Center (ITRC)

One of the strategies of WVCOM International in reaching our goal of " Declaring the Gospel of the Kingdom, Unveiling the Purposes of God and Impacting the Nations"; is to build and establish an International Training & Resource Centre (ITRC). A multi–purpose facility that will serve as a base for the WV-COM International office, a 500 seater training/conference hall, media studio, Christian library, offices for our international network partners around the nations, and for our Intercessory Network of Prayers for the nations. It will also provide guest homes for our resident leaders and those in the process of leadership training, and as well serve for Community Development & Empowerment Programs to impact the communities through humanitarian services to the less privileged.

The International Training & Resource Centre (ITRC) will offer the opportunity for leadership training, assistance in the five-fold ministry gifts, conferences/seminars and consulting services.

ITRC will become a prototype Antioch Centre to release matured leaders and ministries into the nations. First, a place of identifying emerging leaders for training and development; and for those already in ministry wanting to make a transition from 'church' to 'kingdom' - a paradigm shift into a new concept of kingdom lifestyle and transitioning from the old strategy of church system to an innovative concept of the kingdom. It is a process of change of the old wineskin for the new, by creating an environment for impartation and development to assist leaders and ministries to make full transition into a kingdom dimension in the present move of God.

ITRC will teach, train, mentor, mature, and activate gifts and ministries. We will impart, develop, motivate and release leaders and the saints to understanding personal calling and identifying their gifts and talents, so they can function in their God ordained ministry in fulfilling the purposes of God.

ITRC will help disciple, deepen and strengthen the relationship of the leaders with God through the impartation of knowledge and experience with biblical principles. ITRC will function and operate as a resource and networking centre, bringing together leaders and ministries around the world of like vision and purpose in order to see the kingdom of God established in the earth. Our desire is that from this centre there will be an effective networking, church planting and follow up of leaders and the release of the five-fold ministry as a team and company to the nations.

This is the strategy of WVCOM International to fulfill the vision and mandate of God upon our lives, and we are praying and trusting the Father that this will become a reality. We trust the Lord for the finances to build this facility for the kingdom of God.

The cost is enormous, but the impact is invaluable.

We humbly ask that you prayerfully consider being in partnership with this assignment through your financial support. Churches and ministries around the nations, who are interested to see the kingdom of God advance through this ministry, can contribute to this project.

About The Author

Israel Onoriobe is the Founder and International Administrator of the World Vision Crusade Outreach Ministries (WVCOM International), an apostolic kingdom reformation ministry charged with the mandate of 'Declaring the Gospel of the Kingdom, Unveiling the Purposes of God & Impacting the Nations'.

Born in Benin City, Nigeria he got save in 1990 at the age of 15, and began ministry in 1993 at the tender age of 18. He was set apart and commissioned as an apostle by John M. Boney who is the apostolic overseer of the Emmanuel Ministries International (EMI), along with other apostolic leaders.

World Vision Crusade Outreach Ministries (WVCOM International) was founded in response to a God given vision for the last day Church and World Harvest. Cooperating with the great outpouring of the Holy Spirit, WVCOM International seeks the release and development of our Lord's glorious Church.

Brother Israel travels extensively around the nations of the different continents ministering the message of the kingdom and declaring the purposes of God in releasing the Body of Christ into a greater maturity and Christ-like stature. He has ministered in over 44 nations.

In the last decade, an apostolic commission was released upon this work to see a cooperative networking of churches, ministries and ministers who would give themselves in a greater expression of apostolic release.

Flowing out of this have come a new fresh fire of revelation, restoration and revival power. Signs, wonders, and miraculous healings are being preached and demonstrated. A great hunger for the impartation of healing and restoration within the Body has emerged. Brother Israel has seen an unprecedented volume of healing and restoration being released during his time of ministry, and many have also been delivered from demonic strongholds and oppressions.

Brother Israel fully believes a new move of the Spirit is upon the nations that will lead to an unprecedented ingathering, shaping and changing the face of the Church.

World Vision Crusade Outreach Ministries have become an active cog in the wheel of Kingdom Building, Kingdom Advancement and Kingdom Excellence in Africa and beyond. In the last few years, WVCOM International has been instrumental in changing Church cultures and facilitating change in ministries – causing a paradigm shift into a new concept of kingdom lifestyle and transitioning from the old strategy (church) to an innovative concept (kingdom). It is a change of the old wineskin for the new.

We have also been involved in setting up the 'Kingdom Advancement Leadership Summit' and training seminars for Church leaders over the years in different nations. This is one of the principle aims of WVCOM International: to teach, train and to release new kingdom workers as well as ordain new leadership with apostolic commissions. This we believe will be accomplished through establishing of covenant relationships and partnership with other like ministries and leaders across the nations, as the Lord divinely bring the links together for His purpose.

WVCOM International does serve to bring covering for orphan ministries, churches and ministers, to relate in a covenant relationship and proclamation for kingdom advancement for the reformation and restoration of all things. With this, we solely proclaim and declare that WVCOM International mission is to provide a relational network of ministries and churches that are in vital covenant relationships with one another. This comes about through a united vision of equipping, releasing and maturing the Church. The core of the vision is to see existing churches strengthened, new churches planted, global missions and evangelism, and the training of ministry leadership. The purpose is to see the Body of Christ come into her Glory for the fullness of Christ's stature awaiting His appearance.

By a passion to advance the kingdom of God, WVCOM International is seeking those who have heard such a call in the Spirit. We are labouring to enter into functional relationship with those who are called to bring restoration and apostolic reformation to the Church by every possible means necessary.

Brother Israel is presently based in Cape Town, South Africa with his wife, Miliswa and their daughter, Destiny from where they oversee the work of the ministry into the nations.

Ministry Booking

To Invite The Author To Speak At A Conference,
A local Church or City/Nation, Please Contact Us At:

World Vision Crusade Outreach Ministries
9 Pegasus Road,
Milnerton, Cape Town 7441
South Africa

Tel: +27 (0)21-828-2345
Mobile: +27 (0)82-228-9180
Email: wvcom2001@yahoo.com
Website: www.wvcom-international.org

Other Books By The Author:

Apostolic Strategies for Kingdom Reformation – Series 1
Apostolic Strategies for Kingdom Reformation – Series 2
Apostolic Strategies for Kingdom Reformation – Series 3
The Process of Transition
The Way of the Wilderness

These books can be ordered as a hard copy by contacting the ministry office, or as an e-Book online our website. Other teaching materials, audios and articles can also be seen online our ministry website:

Visit Us Online
@
www.wvcom-international.org

93768713R00089

Made in the USA
Columbia, SC
19 April 2018